A PHOTOGRAPHIC GUIDE TO

TREES

OF

NEW ZEALAND

LAWRIE METCALF

D1419997

Dedicated to my wife, Lena, who is not only very patient and understanding while I work on books, but is always of invaluable assistance, particularly with helping to find the best specimens to photograph, whilst on our photographic travels around the country, and who is also such a wonderful friend and companion.

First published in 2002 by New Holland Publishers (NZ) Ltd
Auckland • Sydney • London • Cape Town

218 Lake Road, Northcote, Auckland, New Zealand
Unit 1, 66 Gibbes Street, Chatswood, NSW 2067, Australia
86–88 Edgware Road, London W2 2EA, United Kingdom
80 McKenzie Street, Cape Town 8001, South Africa

www.newhollandpublishers.co.nz

Copyright © 2002 in text: Lawrie Metcalf
Copyright © 2002 in photography: Lawrie Metcalf
Copyright © 2002 New Holland Publishers (NZ) Ltd

ISBN: 978 1 877246 57 9

Publishing manager: Matt Turner
Design and typesetting: Julie McDermid
Editor: Brian O'Flaherty

Colour reproduction by Pica Digital Pte Ltd, Singapore
Printed by Times Offset (M) Sdn Bhd, Malaysia, on paper sourced from
sustainable forests.

10 9 8

Front cover photograph: cabbage tree (*Cordyline australis*), courtesy of Philip
Simpson, from his book *Dancing Leaves: the story of New Zealand's cabbage
tree Ti Kouka*, Canterbury University Press, 2000. © Philip Simpson.
Back cover photograph: rata (*Metrosideros robusta*).
Spine photograph: akeake (*Dodonaea viscosa*).
Title page photograph: mountain ribbonwood (*Hoheria glabrata*).

Contents

Introduction

The usual definition of a tree is that it is a large, woody perennial plant having a distinct trunk with branches at some distance from the ground. While many trees may fit that definition, it is also true that many smaller trees often have several trunks arising from ground level, as well as branches close to the ground. Thus, there is often a considerable overlap between trees and shrubs and it may then be difficult to decide whether a particular plant is a small tree or a large shrub. The situation is further complicated by the fact that when some larger trees grow in exposed and open situations they often behave as shrubs.

To the old-time Maori inhabitants of New Zealand, the trees of the forests were considered to be the children of Tane, the god of the forests. If it was desired to cut down a tree for any purpose, such as building a canoe, it was firstly necessary to placate Tane with the appropriate karakia, or prayers. After the tree was felled it was also the custom to replace it with a seedling of the same species.

When the European colonists arrived in New Zealand, the forests were viewed as a vast and, seemingly, limitless resource of material for building and other purposes. These dense forests were also regarded as something that had to be conquered if the settlers were to establish themselves in this new land, to create farms and towns that would provide them with their livelihoods. Fortunately, this attitude has largely changed so that most people now have a greater respect and understanding of our native forests and trees, and their place in the natural environment.

Before any humans settled in this country, it is estimated that some 83 per cent of the land was covered with forest. By the beginning of the 19th century, just prior to the advent of European colonisation, the forest cover had been reduced to about 64 per cent, and, over the last 160 years, the forest cover has been reduced to only about 23 per cent.

Each species in this guide is described in easily understood terms and illustrated with one or more photographs. Wherever possible, juvenile forms have also been illustrated. Habitat notes and distributions are included, while Maori and other usages are also given, where appropriate.

How to use this book

In order to assist users to identify the plants illustrated, a simple key has been provided on pages 12–13. At first glance it may appear to be complicated, but with a little practice you will find that it is quite easy to use. Instructions for the key are on page 11.

Headings

Although common names are highlighted for ease of reference, all plants are listed according to their scientific names so that their affinities with related species may easily be seen. The scientific names are those in current use although, given the amount of research into New Zealand botany, it is quite possible that some names may well be superseded within a short space of time. The common names given are those that are generally recognised. Some species do not have recognised common names, and so the temptation to use pretentious, coined names has been resisted. Both common names and scientific names are listed in the index.

The family to which each species belongs is also given. Family names appear in the coloured tabs in the top margin of each page.

The trees described

Most of the trees described, and illustrated, are the commoner species that are more likely to be seen when journeying around various parts of New Zealand. They are listed according to their various families, which are in currently accepted botanical order, while the members of each family (genus and species) are grouped together so that it is possible to compare them with related species. For ease of finding, the genera and species of each family group are arranged in alphabetical order.

Practically all of New Zealand's trees are evergreen and there are fewer than about 12 species that may be classed as being deciduous. Of those, some may be deciduous only at flowering time (the *Sophora* species), while one or two others are only deciduous in the colder parts of the country or when growing at higher altitudes.

When attempting to identify a tree in the wild, firstly try to do so with the aid of the key, and then compare it with the description and accompanying illustration. Each description includes the main characters necessary for identifying the particular species. Some are quite obvious and may be identified from the illustration alone, but others may also need to be checked against the description. For final confirmation, check it against the distribution map.

Terminology

In all descriptions an attempt has been made to keep botanical terminology to a minimum, but it has not been possible to completely avoid the use of such terms. Sometimes it is for greater accuracy and sometimes to avoid using wordy phrases that can better be expressed by one word. A glossary of the terms used has been provided on pages 122–125 so that readers can learn the meanings of those terms.

Distribution maps

The distribution maps, with each species, indicate the broader areas (in green shading) over which a species may be present. They do not necessarily imply that a particular species will occur in every part of the area indicated. Some species have remarkably discontinuous distributions while, depending upon the part of the country, there may also be considerable distances between one sighting of a particular species and another.

The vegetation of New Zealand

The native trees of New Zealand occur not only in many different species, representing a wide range of plant families, but they also exist in a wide variety of often perplexing forms. Many species undergo a distinct juvenile stage and, with some, the juveniles differ so greatly from the adult that to the uninitiated they may appear to belong to completely different species. In addition, there is often considerable variation in the general appearance of species from one region to another. Such regional variation may be quite marked.

New Zealand's forests differ from practically all others in one important aspect. They evolved and developed into their present form and composition in the complete absence of browsing mammals. Only some species of the, now extinct, large ratite birds (moa) browsed in the forests and they do not appear to have had any marked influence.

Nowadays, the destructive effects of introduced browsing mammals, such as deer, goats, wallabies and brush-tailed possums, have greatly altered the nature and composition of many of the indigenous forests.

New Zealand's forests are broadly classified as rainforests, and are divided into two classes: subtropical rainforest (known as rainforest proper) and subantarctic rainforest. The existence of rainforest is determined by a high rainfall and large number of rainy days per annum. In this respect, they are quite distinct from the forests of more temperate countries, and belong to the same types of rainforest as those of tropical lands.

Apart from the far north of New Zealand, where the climate is subtropical, most of New Zealand's climate is now warm temperate to temperate. However, that does not alter the fact that the rainforest proper is fundamentally of a subtropical nature.

Subtropical rainforest

This includes a mixture of coniferous trees and broad-leaved evergreens. The coniferous trees mainly belong to the Podocarpaceae (commonly known as podocarps), an ancient plant family originating from the former supercontinent of Gondwanaland. Generally, they are tall trees that are either closely placed to form an upper canopy, or they may be more scattered and are then known as emergent trees. The dominance of the various podocarp species gives the forest a very ancient and primeval aspect.

A number of the taller trees often develop buttresses at the bases of their trunks, with their uppermost roots extending, half buried or even raised above the ground, for quite some distance. This is a character typical of many trees of tropical origin. The larger trees usually support a variety of high-perching epiphytes, often thick-stemmed lianes, orchids, mosses, liverworts and ferns. Tree ferns are often abundant in many areas.

The whole aspect of New Zealand's subtropical rainforest is that of a mountain forest in countries such as New Guinea,

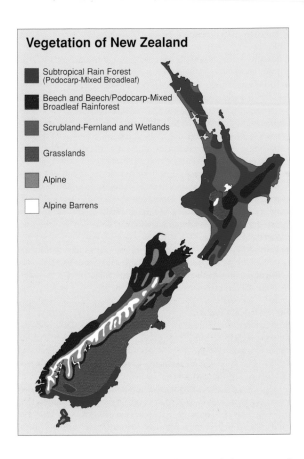

Vegetation of New Zealand

- Subtropical Rain Forest (Podocarp-Mixed Broadleaf)
- Beech and Beech/Podocarp-Mixed Broadleaf Rainforest
- Scrubland-Fernland and Wetlands
- Grasslands
- Alpine
- Alpine Barrens

Indonesia or the Philippines. Formerly, it extended over most of the North Island and throughout much of the South Island, apart from the dry eastern areas of Marlborough, Canterbury, and northern and central Otago. Stewart Island is still mostly forested. From north to south there is a progressive drop-out of some of the less hardy species, while in north-west Nelson and the Marlborough Sounds there is an interesting overlap with a number of typically North Island species occurring in those areas.

In New Zealand's subtropical rainforest a number of distinct forest types may occur. Some of the main ones are:

- **Kauri forest**, which once covered much of the northern part of the North Island from Kawhia and the Coromandel to the far north, would probably be the most notable. Although kauri (*Agathis*) is the dominant tree, taraire (*Beilschmiedia tarairi*) is also a conspicuous component, in addition to other mixed trees and shrubs.

- **Tawa forest**, in which the tawa (*Beilschmiedia tawa*) is one of the main trees. It occurs rather locally in various parts of the North Island and also in the Marlborough Sounds area of the South Island.
- **Kahikatea forest** is quite distinct from all other forest types. It occurs mainly in wet alluvial ground or shallow swamps, and it receives its name from the fact that kahikatea (*Dacrycarpus dacrydioides*) is the dominant tree. At times kahikatea may be completely dominant, or almost to the exclusion of other tall trees. It was formerly common in areas such as the Waikato, the King Country and Westland.
- **Northern rata forest** receives its name from the fact that *Metrosideros robusta* is a conspicuous component of such forest. The massive rata trees often support large aerial gardens of epiphytic and climbing forest species. As well as occurring in the North Island it also occurs in parts of Nelson and northern Westland.
- **Kamahi forest** is dominated by *Weinmannia racemosa* and particularly occurs in parts of Westland and Stewart Island. It can often occur after there has been partial forest clearance when kamahi seedlings quickly invade open spaces in the forest.

Subantarctic rainforest

This rainforest is characterised by the presence of the various species of *Nothofagus* or southern beech, and is generally of a more temperate nature. These beech forests are remarkably uniform in composition, and they extend from the southern part of the Coromandel Peninsula (with the exception of *N. truncata* which extends as far north as Mangonui) to Southland. Strangely, the beeches are absent from Stewart Island. In general, they follow the mountain ranges but some species are also common in lowland areas. Particularly in the southern part of their range, as well as in the Marlborough Sounds, they also occur down to sea level. The beeches are light-demanding species and usually form such a dense canopy that the range of other species, growing inside the forest, is often rather limited.

In various areas mixed associations of subtropical and subantarctic rainforests may occur, or the *Nothofagus* often occurs on the more barren slopes and ridges while the podocarp/mixed broadleaf forest occupies the moister and more fertile soils in the gullies.

Scrublands

Scrublands are those areas where multi-stemmed shrubs predominate, but they can also integrate with fernlands where bracken fern (*Pteridium esculentum*) and possibly tangle fern (*Gleichenia*) dominate. In lowland and hilly areas, scrublands now occur mainly where the original forest cover has been cleared or disturbed. Above the tree line, in mountain areas, there is usually a distinct zone of subalpine scrub. Such scrub is often quite impenetrable.

Grasslands

In New Zealand there are two main kinds of grassland, distinguished as low-tussock grassland and tall-tussock grassland. In them, most of the principal grass species grow as individual clumps or tussocks. These grasslands occur mainly in the drier, low-rainfall regions along the eastern sides of both main islands. The low-tussock grasslands comprise species of *Poa* and *Festuca*, and occur in lowland and hill country areas. The tall-tussock grasslands comprise species of *Chionochloa* (generally known as snow grass or snow tussock) and occur mainly at higher altitudes, except in the far south of the South Island where they descend to sea level.

Alpine areas

Particularly in the South Island, there are extensive alpine areas above the subalpine scrub where a rich variety of alpine vegetation occurs. The North Island has its share of alpine vegetation on the volcanic peaks and higher mountain ranges, while Stewart Island also has a notable alpine vegetation. The alpine vegetation grows in a number of associations or communities varying from snow tussock-herbfield to herbfield, snow tussock grassland, bogs, fellfield and shingle scree. About 71 per cent of New Zealand's alpine species are confined to the South Island. Above 2000–2400 m is the nival zone or the permanent snow line. Only one or two species of alpine plants are able to survive in the nival zone.

Using the key to identify the trees

There are 25 letters, or steps to the key, each giving two choices or answers. As most plants flower only for a limited time each year, flowers have not been used as a means of identification. Consequently, this key is based entirely on leaf and stem characters.

To begin
Always commence at step **A**. Carefully examine the foliage of the tree that you wish to identify and decide which of the two choices best applies to it. Then proceed to whichever step is next indicated (letters on the right-hand side of the page). Continue through the key until you arrive at a number or group of numbers, in **bold type**, which then will refer you to suggested text page numbers. You can then compare your tree with the text and photographs until you find one that matches.

Example
Beginning at **A**. If the tree you want to identify has long spines (thorns) on its branches and branchlets, you should go straight to **text and photograph p. 81**. If it is without spines you are referred to step **B**. This step gives you a choice of '*Leaves small and scale-like, usually less than 5 mm long and tightly pressed around the branchlet*', or '*Leaves larger, not small and scale-like*'. If the tree you are trying to identify has small and scale-like leaves, you are then referred to **pp. 14–18, 27, 28**. This takes you to the conifers and podocarps. If you then refer to those entries it should be possible to match your plant with one of those species.

The second choice for step **B** states: '*Leaves larger, not small and scale-like…C*'. Should that be the case, it is then necessary to go to step **C**. From there on, by a simple process of elimination, you should eventually be able to match your plant with the appropriate text and illustration. The distribution maps with each entry will also help.

Range of use
This key is designed for use on adult trees only and not juvenile forms. It is meant to be only an aid to identification and is not intended to be 100 per cent accurate.

Further, because of regional and habitat variations some trees may not conform to the dimensions given in the key. When measuring leaf dimensions, it is suggested that you use an average from several leaves. Compound leaves are those that arise from one main stalk (petiole) and divide into several larger leaflets (like the fingers of a hand), or have numerous small leaflets arranged either side of a midrib, which is usually an extension of the petiole or main leaf stalk.

Key to the species described

A. Branches and branchlets with long spines (thorns).........**p. 81**

Branches and branchlets without spines.............................**B**

B. Leaves small and scale-like, usually less than 5 mm long and tightly pressed around the branchlet........... **pp. 14–18, 27, 28**

Leaves larger, not small and scale-like................................**C**

C. Leaves simple (e.g. just one single-leaf blade).....................**D**

Leaves compound with several to numerous leaflets...........**M**

D. Margins of leaves smooth (not toothed)..............................**E**

Margins of leaves toothed..**Q**

E. Leaves usually less than 5 cm long......................................**F**

Leaves usually more than 5 cm long.....................................**I**

F. Leaves less than 2.5 cm long..**G**

Leaves more than 2.5 cm long...**H**

G. Leaves very narrow....................................**pp. 19–23, 45, 46**

Leaves rounded...**pp. 48, 74, 75, 99**

H. Leaves narrow, usually less than 2 cm wide.................**pp. 20, 29, 50, 51, 52, 61, 110**

Leaves usually more than 2.5 cm wide.... **pp. 41, 42, 44, 47, 49, 98, 104, 108**

I. Leaves usually more than 20 cm long......**pp. 94, 96, 114, 115**

Leaves usually less than 20 cm long.....................................**J**

J. Leaves usually less than 2.5 cm wide...................................**K**

Leaves usually more than 2.5 cm wide................................**V**

K. Leaves whitish beneath................................ **pp. 43, 107, 108**

Leaves not whitish beneath...**L**

L. Leaves usually less than 1.5 cm wide..............**pp. 38, 95, 103**

Leaves usually more than 1.5 cm wide................**pp. 26, 31, 41, 85, 100–102**

M. Leaflets arranged like the fingers of a hand..........................**N**

Leaflets arranged along a central stalk or midrib................**O**

N. Leaflets toothed around their margins........ **pp. 86, 87, 90, 91**
Leaflets not toothed around their margins............**pp. 82, 112**

O. Leaves very large, fern-like or palm-like,
usually longer than 1 m.................................... **pp. 116–121**
Leaves much smaller, not fern-like or palm-like,
usually less than 50 cm..**P**

P. Leaflets usually very small...............................**pp. 70, 71**
Leaflets usually larger..**Y**

Q. Leaves very large, usually more than 20 x 20 cm............**p. 53**
Leaves much narrower, usually less than 15 cm long...........**R**

R. Leaves usually less than 2.5 cm wide...................................**S**
Leaves usually more than 2.5 cm wide.................................**T**

S. Leaves narrow...................**pp. 35, 55–57, 61, 67, 88, 89, 107**
Leaves rounded....................................**pp. 66, 72, 73, 76, 78**

T. Teeth around margins usually few or
widely spaced.......................**pp. 33, 39, 67– 69, 80, 109, 111**
Teeth around margins numerous
and more closely placed..**U**

U. Young shoots minutely hairy or downy............. **pp. 58–62, 77**
Young shoots smooth,
not hairy or downy..............................**pp. 34, 36, 54, 63, 66**

V. Leaves buff or
whitish beneath......................**pp. 43, 49, 105, 106, 108, 113**
Leaves not buff or whitish beneath....................................**W**

W. Leaves more or less paired..**p. 40**
Leaves not in pairs... **X**

X. Leaves usually not less than 7 cm long........**pp. 30, 42, 79, 93**
Leaves often shorter than 7 cm...................**pp. 32, 37, 92, 97**

Y. Margins of leaflets toothed................... **pp. 24–26, 64, 65, 84**
Margins of leaflets not toothed...............................**p. 40, 83**

Kahikatea *Dacrycarpus dacrydioides* 24–60 m

Kahikatea is the tallest of our forest trees and specimens over 60 m tall have been measured. Its very straight trunk is usually clear of branches for a considerable height. Although formerly one of the commonest of native trees, timber milling and land clearance have greatly reduced its habitats. In spite of that, small groups of young trees are not infrequently seen on some farmlands. It is often the dominant tree in swampy forests or on moist alluvial flats. Kahikatea occurs in lowland forests throughout the North, South and Stewart Islands. As with many New Zealand trees, **juveniles** differ greatly from the adults, and **semi-mature** trees have a distinctly conical shape. The **trunk** is often fluted or buttressed at the base and the dark grey **bark** is more or less smooth, scaling off in flakes. Its **adult leaves** are small and scale-like, sharply pointed and more or less appressed to the branchlets. The small **fruits** consist of a swollen and fleshy, orange footstalk or receptacle, on top of which sits a black seed covered with a waxy bloom. In the autumn they can often be seen on the ground beneath the tree. It is also known as white pine.

Semi-adult trees.

Rimu *Dacrydium cupressinum* 18–30 m

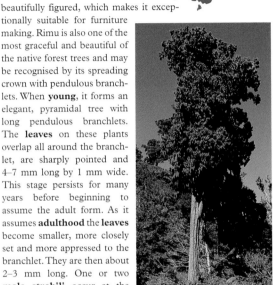

Rimu has been the principal native timber tree, being used for all aspects of house-building, panelling and the manufacture of ply-wood. Its heart-wood is usually beautifully figured, which makes it exceptionally suitable for furniture making. Rimu is also one of the most graceful and beautiful of the native forest trees and may be recognised by its spreading crown with pendulous branchlets. When **young**, it forms an elegant, pyramidal tree with long pendulous branchlets. The **leaves** on these plants overlap all around the branchlet, are sharply pointed and 4–7 mm long by 1 mm wide. This stage persists for many years before beginning to assume the adult form. As it assumes **adulthood** the **leaves** become smaller, more closely set and more appressed to the branchlet. They are then about 2–3 mm long. One or two **male strobili** occur at the branchlet tips. **Female flowers** are solitary. It has a straight **trunk** that may be up to 1.5 m in diameter. The **bark** is dark brownish grey and scaling off in long flakes. Some standing trees are estimated to be 800–1000 years

old. It is a true rainforest tree and in some forests is the main canopy tree, while in others it is more scattered and may be seen only as an emergent tree. Rimu was formerly abundant in lowland and hilly forests throughout the North, South and Stewart Islands, from sea level to 600 m. It was commonly known as red pine.

Semi-adult foliage.

15

Yellow pine *Halocarpus biformis* 3–9 m

Yellow pine is a small tree, often no more than 3–4 m tall. It also occurs in subalpine scrub where it may then be no more than a bushy shrub. A characteristic of this species is that even adult plants will generally display some branchlets with juvenile foliage in addition to the much smaller adult foliage. Its **trunk** may be 30–60 cm in diameter with its greyish **bark** flaking off in small platelets. The cypress-like foliage is tightly appressed around the **branchlets**. The prominently keeled **leaves** are not sharply pointed, and are about 2 mm long. Juvenile reversion shoots usually occur on most adult trees. These leaves spread out from the branchlet and are 8–20 mm long. Yellow pine occurs in mountain and subalpine forests, and scrub, from the Volcanic Plateau of the North Island southwards. It is generally not particularly common in the North Island but is more common along the western side of the South Island and on Stewart Island. Usually occurs from about 600–1370 m.

Adult and juvenile foliage.

Yellow silver-pine *Lepidothamnus intermedius* 15 m

Yellow silver-pine is generally a small tree of a rather spreading habit, often with a yellowish appearance. The **trunk** is usually straight and may be up to 60 cm in diameter. Its **bark** is brownish grey and is shed in small platelets, under which the new bark is a reddish brown. On **juvenile** plants the **leaves** are spreading, 9–15 mm long and more or less flattened in the one plane; those of **semi-adults** tend to spread around the branchlet, becoming shorter and more scale-like. The branchlets of **adult** trees are cypress-like with the scale-like **leaves** being 1.5–3 mm long. They have blunt tips and are more or less arranged around the branchlet in four rows. Its small blackish **seeds** sit among the leaves at the tips of the branchlets. The wood of yellow silver-pine is reddish yellow, very strong and durable. It was formerly used for telegraph poles and railway sleepers. Yellow silver-pine occurs in lowland, montane and subalpine forests. It is scattered in the North Island from the Bay of Islands southwards; in the South Island it occurs mainly on the western side, and on Stewart Island.

Adult foliage.   *Juvenile foliage.*

17

Silver pine *Manoao colensoi* 15 m

Although silver pine is commonly cone-shaped, it is only the semi-mature trees which exhibit that form. Really old and mature trees may have a moderately spreading crown. The **trunk** can be up to 1 m in diameter and the brownish grey **bark** sheds in flakes that first detach from their bottom ends. The **branchlets** are cypress-like, with the **leaves** being about 2.5 mm long, slightly pointed and appressed all around the branchlet. **Juvenile** plants are quite different, the **leaves** being up to 12 mm long and spreading around the branchlet. In the **semi-adult** stage the **leaves** become smaller (about 5 mm long) and are arranged in two opposite rows, in the same plane. Silver pine occurs in lowland to montane forests, in the North Island from near Kaitaia to Mt Ruapehu, and down the western side of the South Island to southern Westland. Its wood is very durable and was formerly used for railway sleepers, telegraph poles and fence posts. *Manoao* was formerly in the genus *Lagarostrobus*.

Needle-leaved totara *Podocarpus acutifolius* 4–9 m

Needle-leaved totara has one of the most restricted distributions of the native podocarps, being confined to the South Island where it occurs from the Marlborough Sounds to Nelson and then down the western side of the island to south Westland. It is always a small tree, no more than 9 m tall, and quite often only a spreading, bushy shrub. It is easily recognised by its straight and narrow **leaves** that are needle-pointed. They are 1.5–2.5 cm long and no  more than 3.5 mm wide. When growing in open situations the foliage is usually a distinctive yellow-green in colour, but in more sheltered habitats it is usually green. When it forms a tree, the **trunk** may be up to 50 cm in diameter and has thin **bark** that peels off in short strips or flakes. Its nut-like **seeds** are green when ripe and sit on top of a red and swollen, succulent receptacle.

Hall's totara is closely related to totara but is most easily distinguished by its thin and rather papery **bark** as opposed to the tough, thick and fibrous bark of totara. Usually its foliage is larger than that of totara, but that is not always a well-defined character. Hall's totara makes quite a large tree and with a rather thick **trunk** up to 1.25 m in diameter. Its **leaves** are 2–3 cm long by 3–4 mm wide, and sharply pointed. On **juvenile** plants they are noticeably larger and may be up to 5 cm long. The pollen is produced from **strobili** up to 2.5 cm long, which fall from the tree soon after the

pollen has been shed. The **female flowers** are produced singly or in pairs. The nut-like **seeds** are green when ripe and are produced from the top of a red and swollen, succulent receptacle. Hall's totara is often known as thin-bark totara. It occurs in lowland, mountain and lower subalpine forests from Northland, and throughout the South and Stewart Islands. Hall's totara bark was formerly used by southern Maori to encase the kelp bags used for storing muttonbirds. These containers are known as pohatiti.

Adult foliage.

Juvenile foliage.

Totara *Podocarpus totara* 30 m

One of the largest trees in the forest, its timber was prized by Maori as being the best for building their massive war canoes, and was also the main timber used for carving. Until more recent times it was also valued for bridge and wharf construction, as well as a wide variety of other uses. The totara grows into a large tree, with a massive **trunk** up to 2 m or more in diameter, with the largest specimens being 3 m or more.

Younger trees have densely bushy crowns, but with age the crown becomes more open. Its **bark** is thick and fibrous, often deeply furrowed and quite stringy. The **leaves** vary from a dull brownish green (on juveniles) to a dark green and are usually 1.5–3 mm long by 3–4 mm wide. They are straight to slightly curved and pungently pointed. The **strobili** are up to 2 cm long, solitary or up to four together. The female **flowers** are solitary or in pairs and the nut-like **seeds** (green when ripe) are produced from the top of a red or orange, swollen and succulent receptacle. Totara is common in lowland, mountain and lower subalpine forests from the far north of the North Island to the south of the South Island. At higher altitudes its place is often taken by *P. hallii*. Ancient Maori custom demanded that when a totara tree was felled for timber a young seedling had to be planted in its place in order to appease Tane, the god of the forest, for removing one of his 'children'.

Miro *Prumnopitys ferruginea* 25 m

Miro is a widespread tree, appearing in forest areas throughout the length and breadth of the country. It occurs in lowland and lower mountain forests up to an altitude of 900 m. The timber is hard, straight-grained and often beautifully figured. It was commonly used for flooring, house building and general carpentry. Miro grows into a round-headed tree with a **trunk** up to 1 m in diameter. The **bark** is a dark grey or grey-brown

and falls off in thick flakes. The **leaves** are 1.5–2.5 cm long by 2–3 mm wide (**juveniles** differ only in their longer leaves), dark green and are arranged along the branchlets in the one plane. The **male strobili** are about 1.5 cm long and are produced from the leaf axils. The solitary (occasionally paired) **female flowers** are produced on short branchlets, and the **fruits** take more than 12 months to ripen. When ripe, the drupaceous fruits (covered with a waxy bloom) are up to 2 cm long and are a purplish red.

Matai is one of the numerous New Zealand trees that goes through a distinct juvenile stage during which it bears little resemblance to the adult. **Juvenile** plants have a divaricating habit with slender and flexuous interlacing branches and rather sparse brownish foliage. This juvenile stage lasts for many years before the tree gradually changes into the adult. When mature it forms a tree with a **trunk** up to 1.3 m in diameter. The **bark** is dark grey and is shed in thick, rounded plates. One of the tree's distinguishing characters is the way in which the bark is shed to give the trunk a hammer-marked appearance. At the time of spring growth, in particular, the newly exposed areas of bark are quite reddish. The **adult leaves** are 1–1.5 cm long by 1–2 mm wide, dark green above, rather glaucous below and have blunt tips. Male and female flowers are borne on separate trees. The **male strobili** are produced in spikes (3–5 cm long) of 10–30 per spike. The **female flowers** are also produced in spikes, about 4 cm long, with three to 10 per spike. The drupaceous **fruits** take about 12 months to ripen. They are globose, about 1 cm in diameter, blackish when ripe and with a waxy bloom. Matai lives to a great age and one tree, in south Westland, is estimated to be more than 1000 years old. Matai was formerly known as black pine.

Mountain toatoa *Phyllocladus aspleniifolius* var. *alpinus* 9 m

Mountain toatoa comprises one or two distinct entities. One grows in forests and is a small tree, while in mountain areas it often inhabits subalpine scrub and is usually only a bushy shrub about 2 m, or less, tall. It is quite aromatic when damaged or bruised. The **trunk** may be up to 40 cm in diameter and the medium to lightish grey **bark** has a slightly warty and wrinkled appearance. *Phyllocladus* are distinct because they do not have true leaves (except as very small seedlings) and have flattened stems, known as phylloclades, that look like and perform the functions of leaves. The **phylloclades** are quite thick and leathery and are of various shapes from more or less diamond-shaped to spoon-shaped. Usually they are up to 2.5 cm long, but on younger plants and some adult forms they

may be much longer. Their margins are irregularly toothed. The **male strobili** are produced from the tips of the branchlets in clusters of two to five. The **females** arise along the margins of the phylloclades or on their stalks. Mountain toatoa occurs on subapline and mountain forests from Cape Colville and Te Aroha in the North Island, and throughout the South Island. It usually ranges from 450–1520 m. In Westland and Southland it descends to sea level.

Toatoa *Phyllocladus toatoa* 15 m

Toatoa is the most striking of the New Zealand species of *Phyllocladus* and is easily recognised because it is so distinct from the two other species. The **phylloclades** are pinnately arranged on a central stalk or rachis 10–30 cm long. They are much larger than those of the other species, thick and leathery, and usually a bronze colour. Toatoa generally forms a handsome tree and the **trunk** may be up to 60 cm in diameter. The **bark** is greyish with a somewhat warty

appearance and has short horizontal ridges running around it. The **male strobili** are in clusters of 10–20 at the tips of the branchlets. The **female flowers** form globose heads of four to seven together on modified phylloclades springing from towards the bases of the rachides. Toatoa is confined to the north of the North Island, where it occurs in lowland and mountain forests from Mangonui to just south of Rotorua. It ranges from sea level to about 600 m. It was formerly known as *P. glaucus*.

PODOCARPACEAE

Phyllocladus trichomanoides is distinguished from *P. toatoa* by its much smaller phylloclades, which are pinnately arranged on a rachis, and are not nearly as large nor as tough and leathery. It forms a handsome and graceful tree with a **trunk** up to 1 m in diameter. **Young trees** have a pyramidal form, but **older trees** generally have a more spreading appearance. The **bark** is usually smooth and lightish grey, although lichen growth may give it a patchy appearance. The **phylloclades** are 1.2–2.5 cm long, green and there are nine to 15 on a rachis that varies from 2.5–7.5 cm long. The **male strobili** are 8–12 mm long, in terminal clusters of five to 10. The **female flowers** are produced in clusters on the margins of modified phylloclades, near the tips of the branchlets. Its wood is yellowish white, strong and durable, and very elastic. Formerly, it was used for making fishing rods and has even been used for bridge building. The bark is very rich in tannin and Maori used to obtain a red dye from it. Tanekaha is also known as celery pine.

Mountain cedar *Libocedrus bidwillii* 20 m

Mountain cedar is a handsome and very distinctive tree that can be recognised even from some distance. Young plants have a very narrow habit of growth, while mature trees have a narrowly cone-shaped habit with their dark green foliage tending to form distinctively billowing masses. These older trees usually rise for a considerable height on long bare trunks. The almost papery **bark** is shed in narrow, thin strips.

The **branchlets** of **young plants** are flattened and resemble those of *L. plumosa*, but are narrower. The **leaves** are about 3 mm long. The **branchlets** of **adult** trees are quite different. The small scale-like **leaves** are about 2 mm long and are arranged all around the branchlet to give it a slightly square appearance. **Male strobili** are about 7–11 mm long, borne singly at the tips of short branchlets. **Female cones** are about 7–8 mm long, and are composed of four scales. They become woody when ripe. Mountain cedar is not uncommon in the wetter montane and subalpine forests in the North Island from Te Aroha mountain southwards, and in the South Island where it is quite uncommon on the eastern side and more common west of the Main Divide. Usually occurs from about 250–1200 m, but descending to lowland forests in Westland. It is also known as pahautea.

Kawaka *Libocedrus plumosa* 25 m

This graceful tree occurs in lowland and hilly forests, in the North Island from Mangonui to about Rotorua and northern Taranaki. In the South Island it just gains a foothold in north-west Nelson between Colling-wood and West Wanganui Inlet. Its altitudinal range is from sea level to about 600 m. Its **trunk** may have a diameter of 1.2 m. The **bark** is stringy and falls away in long, narrow strips. On **juvenile** trees the **branchlets** are up to 7 mm wide

and quite flattened. On **adult** trees they are narrower, about 3 mm wide and not quite so flattened. The **leaves** are triangular and those that project out from the sides of the branchlets are up to 4 mm long, while those that are flattened along the upper and lower sides are only 1–2 mm long. The **male strobili** are 4–7 mm long and are produced from the tips of short branchlets. The **female cones** are about 1.2 cm long with four scales and, when ripe, become woody. Kawaka wood is dark red with darker streaks and is very durable. It was formerly used for roofing shingles and general building purposes. *Libocedrus plumosa* is also known as kaikawaka or New Zealand cedar.

Kauri *Agathis australis* 30 m

Besides being the noblest of our forest trees the kauri is probably the most famous. Mature kauri trees contain very large volumes of timber and, by world standards, it is regarded as one of the largest of trees. Its wood formerly held first place among New Zealand's timbers. Maori used to build their huge war canoes, capable of holding about 100 warriors, from a single kauri trunk. During the last century it was prized for ship's spars and was extensively used for boat building, general house building and furniture and joinery. The **trunk** of a mature kauri rises tall and straight with very little taper, and may be about 18 m to the first branch. It may average 3 m in diameter, while specimens up to 6 m or more have been measured. The **bark** is a bluish grey and falls off in large, thick flakes. Except for young trees the kauri has a large, spreading crown. On **adult** trees its thick, leathery **leaves** are up to 4 cm long, but are larger on **juvenile** trees. The **cones** are more or less globose, 5–7.5 cm in diameter and when ripe the scales fall away from the central axis. Kauri occurs in lowland and hilly forests from near North Cape to about Kawhia and the Bay of Plenty.

LAURACEAE

With its straight trunk and fine, bold foliage taraire is a distinctive and handsome tree. It is found in coastal, lowland and lower hill forests of the North Island, from near North Cape to Raglan and the East Cape districts, and was a common understorey tree in the kauri forests. It is often local to the south of Auckland. It occurs from sea level to 360 m. The trunk of the taraire may be up to 1 m in diameter. Its **bark** is dark brown and smoothish apart from some pitting. The **branchlets** are densely clad with velvety, rusty-brown fine hairs. Its large, handsome **leaves** are 7.5–15 cm long by 3.2–8.2 cm wide. They are rather thick and tough, and the upper surface is dark green and shining. When very young they are covered with fine, rusty-brown hairs. The small, greenish **flowers** are borne on panicles up to about 6.3 cm long, and are followed by plum-like **fruits** that turn dark, blackish purple when ripe. Flesh of the fruit is not very palatable and has been seldom eaten. Maori steamed the kernels in an umu (oven) for about two days before eating them.

Tawa *Beilschmiedia tawa* 25 m

Tawa is a fast-growing tree, recognised by its erect habit and the graceful manner in which its willow-like foliage hangs from its branchlets. It is a tall tree, with a **trunk** up to 1.2 m in diameter. Its **bark** is smooth, of an even texture, and of a darkish colour. The **leaves** are 5–10 cm long by 1–3 cm wide and are a light yellow-green in colour. The young leaves and branchlets are usually covered with fine silky hairs. The small, greenish **flowers** are borne in panicles up to about 8 cm long that arise from the axils of the branchlets. Its **fruits** are about 2.5 cm long, dark purple and ripen in the late summer to early autumn. Tawa is common in lowland and lower montane forests throughout the North Island, and in the South Island as far south as Westport and the Clarence River. It occurs from sea level to 760 m. As with the taraire, the kernels of the tawa fruits were cooked and eaten by Maori. The long and straight-grained timber was formerly used for making their long bird spears.

Mangeao *Litsea calicaris* 12 m

This small tree is confined to the upper half of the North Island, where it is distributed from North Cape to Mokau on the west and East Cape on the east, from sea level to 600 m. It is not uncommon in forests and favours rich soils. The wood is tough, strong and elastic, and was formerly used for cooperage and for wheel making, but has never been available in any quantity. Mangeao is a closely branched leafy tree and its **trunk** can be 45–80 cm in diameter. The **bark** is a dark, greyish brown. The alternate **leaves** are 5–12.5 cm long by 3.2–5 cm wide. The young leaves are attractively tinted brown or reddish, and when mature are a dull green or yellow-green, often with a slightly marbled appearance. They are often glaucous beneath. Its small, greenish yellow, sweetly scented **flowers** are borne in umbels. There are separate male and female flowers on the same tree. They are produced from the leaf axils, towards the tips of the branchlets, and are followed in late summer by blackish purple **drupes** about 2 cm long.

Pigeonwood *Hedycarya arborea* 12 m

Pigeonwood is a medium-sized tree common in lowland and montane forests on the Three Kings Islands, throughout the North Island and in the warmer parts of the South Island as far south as Banks Peninsula, on the east, and to northern Fiordland on the west. It is found from sea level to about 760 m. The **trunk** of the pigeonwood may be up to 50 cm in diameter. Its **leaves** are thick and leathery, 5–12.5 cm long by

2–5 cm wide and are dark green and shining above. Their margins are coarsely and distantly toothed. The greenish male and female **flowers** are on separate trees and are produced on many-flowered, branched racemes that arise from the leaf axils. The male flowers are 8–12 mm in diameter, and the female flowers are slightly smaller. They have an aromatic scent. The **fruits** are a bright orange to orange-red drupe about 1.5 cm long. They occur in clusters of up to 10. They are a favourite food of the native pigeon. Pigeonwood is sometimes known as porokaiwhiri.

MONIMIACEAE

Pukatea is a tall forest tree and may often be distinguished by the prominent, plank-like root buttresses that often form at the base of its trunk. It most often grows in damp or wet places. The wood is strong and tough. The **trunk** is clean and straight, without branches, for a considerable height, and on very large specimens can be up to 1.8 m in diameter. Its **bark** is usually very pale. Generally, the main **branches** are fairly erect and rather open. The branchlets are distinctly four-angled and, if examined closely, are sparsely hairy when young. The **leaves** are thick and leathery, and 4–7.5 cm long by 2.5–5 cm wide. They are glossy and dark green above, and paler beneath. Their margins are coarsely and bluntly serrate. The small **flowers** are greenish yellow and, on the same tree, may

be perfect or separately male and female. They are produced from the leaf axils, in racemes up to 3 cm long. Pukatea grows in swampy and semi-swampy forests and damp gullies, in lowland districts, throughout the North Island and in the South Island from Marlborough to Nelson and, on the west side, as far south as Fiordland. It grows from sea level to about 600 m.

Mahoewao *Melicytus lanceolatus* 6 m

This small tree is easily distinguished by its bright green, willow-like leaves that are finely toothed around their margins. Mahoewao forms a round-headed tree, with rather erect main branches and its **trunk** may be up to 30 cm in diameter. Its **bark** is frequently a whitish colour. The **leaves** are 7.5–15 cm long by 4 mm–3 cm wide with finely, but bluntly, toothed margins. It is dioecious (male and female flowers on separate trees) and its small, mainly yellowish **flowers** are produced in clusters of two to six, either from the leaf axils or lower down on the bare branchlets. Sometimes the petals of the flowers are purplish. Its blue-black or dark purple berries are about 7 mm long and generally ripen during March and April. Mahoewao is not uncommon in lowland to montane forests and forest margins from about Kaitaia southwards in the North Island, and throughout the South and Stewart Islands. In the South Island it is found mainly west of the Main Divide. It occurs from sea level to about 900 m. Mahoewao is sometimes also known as kai-weta.

VIOLACEAE

Mahoe or whiteywood, as it is often known, is one of the commonest trees in forest areas throughout the country, except in much of Southland where its place is taken by *M. lanceolatus*. It also occurs as a regenerative tree in scrublands. It is found in lowland and montane forests from sea level to about 900 m. In the past, in dry seasons, the foliage has been used as cattle fodder. Mahoe wood was used by pre-European Maori for generating fire by fiction. It generally has a number of main branches, and its **bark** is distinctively whitish. The **leaves** are 5–15 cm long by 3–5 cm wide and are usually bright green above and their margins are coarsely toothed.

The small greenish **flowers** are produced in clusters of two to 10 from the leaf axils, and very commonly from along the bare branchlets. The **berries** are about 5 mm in diameter and may vary from violet to a dark blackish purple.

Tree fuchsia *Fuchsia excorticata* 12 m

Tree fuchsia is one of the most easily recognised small trees to be found in forest areas. Its light brown, peeling, papery **bark** identifies it immediately. As the old bark peels off it exposes the even paler young bark beneath. It is especially common around forest margins and in second-growth areas. Often known simply as 'fuchsia', it is common in lowland and lower mountain forests throughout the North, South and Stewart Islands, ranging from sea level to 1060 m. The fuchsia forms a small tree with usually wide-spreading branches and old specimens may have **trunks** up to 45 cm or more in diameter. Its **leaves** are 5–10 cm long by 2.5–5 cm wide, and deep green above, with silvery undersides. The **flowers** are 2–3.2 cm long and are pendant on slender

pedicels up to 15 mm long. They are followed by purple to black **berries** about 1.5 cm long, which are known as konini. In Westland, konini has been universally adopted as the common name for the tree. It is also known as kotukutuku. Tree fuchsia is the largest member of the genus in the world. In colder districts and in high country it is deciduous during winter.

Toru is a small tree which may be recognised by its rather long and narrow, thick and leathery leaves. It has erect growth and is usually much-branched. On old trees the **trunk** may be up to 20 cm or more in diameter. The **leaves** are 10–20 cm long by 8–16 mm wide, deep green and shining above and pointed at their apexes. Its **flowers** are carried on erect, six- to 16-flowered racemes. They are four-parted, yellowish to

yellowish brown, quite fragrant, and are usually produced in October or November. The **fruit** is a drupe about 12–18 cm long and becomes reddish as it ripens. Toru occurs from sea level to 850 m in lowland to montane scrublands of the North Island, from Mangonui to Rotorua and the East Cape district.

Rewarewa *Knightia excelsa* 30 m

Also known as the New Zealand honey-suckle, rewarewa is a common tree in the northern half of New Zealand. It grows in lowland and montane forests throughout the North Island, and in the Marlborough Sounds and D'Urville Island in the South Island. It ranges from sea level to about 850 m. Rewarewa is easily recognised by its tall columnar appearance, and its long and narrow, very leathery leaves. Its **trunk** may be up to 1 m in diameter. The **bark** is dark  brown to almost black and has a fairly smooth appearance. The main **branches** are erect and help to give the tree its distinctive appearance. The young **branchlets** are clad with dark, rusty-brown tomentum. On young trees the **leaves** are 10–25 cm long by about 2–3 cm wide, while those of adult trees are 10–15 cm or more long by 2.5–4 cm wide. Their margins are coarsely toothed and often somewhat undulating. The **flowers** are produced in dense racemes, about 10 cm long, and their perianth segments are coiled into a tangled mass. The wood is very attractively figured and is used for inlay and other ornamental work. Rewarewa is also commonly known as New Zealand honeysuckle because of its nectarous flowers, which are much favoured by native birds.

Tree tutu is one of New Zealand's best-known poisonous plants. It is a widespread small tree and is one of the first plants to appear after land disturbances such as slips and fire. Tutu may have a short **trunk** up to 30 cm in diameter, although it more often has multiple trunks arising from ground level. Its **bark** is dark brown or greyish, and on old trees is usually furrowed. On younger plants it is fluted and marked with distinct lenticels. The **leaves** are 5–8 cm or more long by 4–5 cm wide and are usually in pairs. Its numerous small, greenish **flowers** are produced on racemes 15–20 cm long. The succulent **fruits** are dark purple and are about 4 mm long. Tutu occurs throughout the North, South, Stewart and Chatham Islands, in scrublands, around forest margins and along roadsides. It is poisonous to farm stock and humans. During the spring season its sap is quite poisonous, while in autumn it is the seeds that are most toxic.

Karo *Pittosporum crassifolium* 9 m

With its conspicuous, large seed capsules and thick leathery leaves karo is an easily recognised species. It occurs around coastal areas of the upper half of the North Island from North Cape to Poverty Bay, particularly along streamsides and forest margins and ranges from sea level to about 950 m. It forms a small tree with ascending branches. The **bark** is grey or dark brown. Its **leaves** are 5–7.5 cm long by 2–2.5 cm wide.

They are dark green and shining above and thickly covered with whitish tomentum beneath. The heavily scented **flowers** are bright to dark red, in five- to 10-flowered, terminal umbels. As with all pittosporums the scent is most noticeable during the evenings. It has large **seed capsules** that are up to 3 cm in diameter and have three to four valves.

Lemonwood is a small tree with a **trunk** that may be up to 60 cm in diameter. Often it can be distinguished by its **bark**, which is very pale to almost whitish. Its **leaves** are more or less whorled, 5–12.5 cm long by 2.5–4 cm wide, with undulating margins, and the midrib is very pale. The **flowers** are produced in terminal clusters and are greenish yellow with a sweet, honey-like scent. Flowering is usually during October to December. The **seed capsules** are about 7 mm long, green at first and black when ripe, which usually takes at least 12 months. It occurs in lowland to montane forests in the North and South Islands from sea level to 760 m. Lemonwood is also commonly known as tarata. The name lemonwood derives from the fact that the crushed leaves emit a lemon-like smell.

Pittosporum ralphii 6 m

This species is closely related to *P. crassifoli-um*, but is distinguished by its larger and thinner oblong leaves. It is distributed from Thames southwards to about Wanganui and Dannevirke where it grows around forest margins, along streamsides and in scrubby country. It is a small tree with a **trunk** up to 45 cm in diameter. The **bark** is dark brown or greyish. Its **leaves** are 5–12.5 cm long by 2.5–5 cm wide, dark green and rather dull above and thinly clad with a whitish tomentum beneath. Their margins are flat or somewhat recurved. *Pittosporum ralphii* has reddish **flowers** in terminal, three- to 10-flowered umbels and are followed by large **seed capsules** about 2 cm long.

Kohuhu is one of the commonest trees, being found widely over much of both main islands. It comprises two subspecies: subspecies *tenuifolium* (the typical form) and subspecies *colensoi*. The former is found throughout the North Island and east of the Main Divide in the South Island, while the latter occurs in the North Island from about Kawhia and the Bay of Plenty southwards, and in the South Island west of the Main Divide. They are fairly similar to each other; ssp. *colensoi* being a slightly larger tree with larger leaves, that do not have such distinctly undulating margins as ssp. *tenuifolium*. Both have **trunks** 30–40 cm in diameter. The **bark** is dark brown to almost black and has a roughened surface. The **leaves** are 2.5–6 cm long by 1.6–2.5 cm wide, shining above with the margins barely to strongly undulating (ssp. *colensoi* 5–10 cm long by 2–5 cm wide, dark green and shining above with the margins flat to slightly undulating). The **flowers** are dark reddish purple to almost black and are sweetly scented, especially in the evenings. Kohuhu is also erroneously known as matipo.

Kanuka *Kunzea ericoides* 15 m

Kanuka is a small tree with a **trunk** that may be 30–60 cm in diameter. Its loose and papery **bark** peels off in long strips. The **leaves** are 4–12 mm long by 1–2 mm wide and are produced in clusters or alternately. They are not pungently pointed. The white **flowers** are 3–7 mm in diameter and may be produced singly, but mostly in two- to five-flowered clusters. Usually they smother the tree in great profusion. Kanuka is common throughout the North Island and in the South Island about as far south as the Clutha River, but is absent from Fiordland. It is abundant in lowland to montane scrublands and often forms extensive thickets and transition forests, particularly on formerly forested country. In some parts of the country, particularly Northland, it is known as manuka, but in most other districts kanuka is the generally used common name. Its wood is red, very hard and is commonly used for firewood. It was formerly used by early Maori for making weapons, and by European settlers for wharf piles, wheel spokes, tool handles and fencing.

MYRTACEAE

Manuka is one of the commonest, and best known, small trees in New Zealand. It is found throughout the country in all manner of situations from sea level to about 1370 m and, depending on habitat, may vary from a small tree to a dwarfed mountain shrub less than a metre tall. On old trees the **bark** is brown and is shed in long strips. The **branchlets** are silky with whitish hairs, and its small **leaves** are 4–10 mm long by 2–6 mm wide. They are hard to the touch and usually pungently pointed. Its **flowers** are produced singly from the leaf axils, on short branchlets, and are up to 1.6 cm in diameter. Mostly they are white, but it is not uncommon to find variants that are flushed with pink. Its red-coloured wood is very hard and durable and was used for tool handles and fencing. In early colonial times it was sometimes used for brewing a tea-like drink, and was so used by Captain Cook for preventing scurvy. Manuka is also commonly known as tea-tree and north of Auckland is sometimes known as kahikatoa.

Ramarama is a small tree that prefers the more open parts of the forest and is usually common around forest margins and clearings. It is found in coastal and lowland forests throughout the North Island and in the South Island in northern Nelson and Marlborough. It ranges from sea level to 600 m. Ramarama is easily recognised by its **leaves** having a blistered or puckered appearance. The leaves are 2.5–5 cm long by 2–3 cm wide and are usually yellowish

green to green in colour; in open situations they may be reddish. The solitary **flowers** are produced from the leaf axils and are 1.2 cm in diameter. Usually they are a creamy-white but sometimes may have a rosy flush to them. The dark, reddish purple **berries** become almost black when fully ripe.

Rohutu *Lophomyrtus obcordata* 6 m

A small tree that is distinguished by its smooth bark and small, inverted, heart-shaped leaves. Its **trunk** may be up to 30 cm in diameter. The smooth **bark** peels off in longish strips to expose an irregular pattern of the new, pale greenish white bark intermingled with the older brown bark. The **leaves** are 5–12 mm long and wide and are arranged in opposite pairs or clusters. Their undersurfaces are conspicuously dotted with small oil glands. Its creamy-white **flowers** are produced singly from the leaf axils and are about 7 mm in diameter. The **berry** is 7 mm long and varies from bright to dark red, or dark violet. Rohutu is found in both the North and South Islands from about Ahipara southwards, but is absent from much of Southland. It is local from the East Cape northwards and is often local elsewhere. It occurs in coastal and hilly forests from sea level to 1060 m.

Pohutukawa *Metrosideros excelsa* 21 m

This is one of the most magnificent of New Zealand's flowering trees as well as one that most people regard with a great deal of affection. The pohutukawa grows around coastlines and in coastal forests of the North Island from Cape Reinga to Poverty Bay, on the east coast, and Urenui on the west coast. It also occurs inland around the shores and islets of Lake Taupo as well as other lakes of the Volcanic Plateau. It usually grows into a large and spreading tree. Its **trunk** is from 60 cm to 1.8 m in diameter and usually branches very quickly into a number of large main stems. Its greyish **bark** is thick and stringy, and peels off in long flakes. The thick, leathery **leaves** are 2.5–10 cm long by 1.5–5 cm wide, deep green and shining on their upper surfaces, while the undersurfaces are covered with a dense white tomentum. Its **flowers** vary in colour from a bright to deep crimson and contain copious nectar which is favoured by some native birds and also by native geckos. Pohutukawa is also known as the Christmas tree. Its wood is of great strength and durability and its gnarled and bent branches were formerly favoured for boat building.

MYRTACEAE

Rata is one of the giants of the forest, some old rata trees having massive trunks and huge spreading crowns. Its **trunk** may be from 1–2.4 m in diameter. Its **bark** is thin and falls away in small, rectangular flakes. The thick and leathery **leaves** of the rata are 2.5–5 cm long by 1.5–2 cm wide, and are dark green above and paler beneath. If held up to the light numerous translucent oil glands become visible. The **flowers** vary from brilliant to dull red and are produced in terminal clusters. Rata is abundant in coastal, lowland and hilly forests throughout the North Island and in the northern part of the South Island from western Nelson to just north of Greymouth. It ascends from sea level to about 900 m. Rata is a remarkable tree that frequently, but not invariably, commences life as an epiphyte on another forest tree. It then sends down aerial roots that eventually reach the ground and, at the same time, horizontal side roots grow around the host's trunk until, in time, the host tree's trunk is completely enclosed in that of the rata. It is also known as northern rata.

Southern rata *Metrosideros umbellata* 18 m

With its dense foliage of generally narrower, sharply pointed, dark green and shining leaves the southern rata is readily distinguished from *M. robusta*. In spite of its common name it is distributed in the North Island from near Kaitaia to the Tararua Range, although its distribution may be rare and local. It is common in the South Island, particularly on the West Coast but less so on the eastern side. It also occurs on Stewart Island and as far south as the subantarctic Auckland Islands. In altitude it ranges from sea level to about 1060 m. Southern rata forms a much-branched tree and may have a **trunk** up to 1 m or more in diameter. Its papery **bark** is brown to greyish and peels off in small flakes. The **leaves** are 4–7.5 cm long by 1–2 cm wide. They are thick and leathery and distinctly pointed. Their undersides are dotted with numerous small oil glands. Its brilliant red **flowers** are produced in clusters from the tips of short branchlets. Southern rata may flower well only every three or four years, and between-times flowering may often be sporadic. Its heavy wood is tough and very strong, and has been used for boat building. An alternative name is ironwood.

Swamp maire *Syzygium maire* 15 m

Swamp maire is a small, much-branched tree with a spreading crown. Its **trunk** may be up to 60 cm in diameter and has smooth, pale **bark**. The deep green **leaves** are 4–5 cm long by 1–1.5 cm wide and usually have slightly undulating margins. They are not infrequently disfigured by small blisters. These are the result of their being attacked by a small native insect. Its slightly creamy-white **flowers** are about 12 mm in diameter and are borne in clusters that are up to 8 cm across. The **fruit** is a berry about 12 mm in diameter and is quite a bright red. It takes about 12 months to ripen. Swamp maire is found in lowland swampy and boggy forests throughout

most of the North Island and in Nelson and northern Marlborough in the South Island. It can grow in very wet situations, even with water around the base of its trunk and over the root zone, and may be considered a true swamp-forest tree. In such situations it has been known to produce pneumatophores similar to those of the mangrove. *Syzygium* is a large tropical genus, particularly of South America. The swamp maire was formerly in the genus *Eugenia*. It is also known as maire tawake.

Whau *Entelea arborescens* 6 m

Whau is a handsome and quite distinctive small tree that is easily recognised by its large, soft leaves and bristly or spiny seed capsules. It is not uncommon in coastal and lowland forests as far south as Raglan and the Bay of Plenty, and then rather localised throughout the southern part of the North Island. In the South Island it occurs in coastal localities around Golden Bay, Tasman Bay and the Marlborough Sounds. It is abundant on some of the offshore islands

from the Three Kings down to about Mayor Island. On the mainland it usually grows in sheltered gullies and along the bases of cliffs. Whau will form a small tree and may have a **trunk** up to 25 cm in diameter. Not infrequently it is no more than a large shrub. Its **bark** is inclined to be smooth, but roughened or pitted with lenticels and old branch scars. The **leaves** are on very long petioles and the blade is from 15–25 cm long by 15–20 cm wide. The large, white **flowers** are produced in large clusters and are followed by quite large **seed capsules** that are covered with rigid bristles or spines. The wood of the whau is remarkable for its lightness and was formerly used by Maori for making floats for their fishing nets.

ELAEOCARPACEAE

Wineberry is a handsome and widely distributed tree, and is one of the first to appear after forest has been disturbed. It is a small tree to 10 m tall and has a **trunk** up to 30 cm in diameter. The **bark** of young branchlets is generally red but on older trees it is quite a dark greyish brown to almost black. Its **leaves** are 5–12 cm long by 4–9 cm wide. The usually rose-coloured **flowers** are unisexual and produced in axillary panicles. Its **fruits** are dark red to almost black and about 8 mm in diameter. Wineberry occurs throughout the North, South and Stewart Islands, in lowland and montane forests from sea level to about 1060 m. It is a light-demanding species and is often quite common around forest margins, along roadsides and on disturbed areas. In colonial times its wood was made into charcoal for the manufacture of gunpowder. It is also known as makomako.

Hinau *Elaeocarpus dentatus* 18 m

Hinau is found in lowland forests throughout the North and South Islands from near North Cape to the Catlins River in Otago. It ascends to about 600 m. It is a medium-sized tree and may have a **trunk** up to 90 cm in diameter. Its greyish **bark** is rough and fissured. The **leaves** are 5–10 cm long by 2–4.5 cm wide. On juvenile plants they are longer and narrower. Their margins are bluntly toothed. The 12 mm-diameter **flowers** are borne in racemes 10 cm or more long. Its **fruits** are purple to purplish grey and are up to 1.8 cm long. In olden times the fruits of the hinau were one of the vegetable foods of Maori. They were unpalatable in their raw state and required exten-

sive treatment to prepare them for eating. They were soaked in water for some days and then the flesh was separated from the kernels, skins and bits of stalks, to eventually leave a coarse, greyish white meal. This was formed into large cakes or loaves that were then baked in an umu (earthen oven) for one or two days. The bark of the hinau was also used to prepare a dark, blue-black dye that was much favoured for dyeing garments.

Pokaka *Elaeocarpus hookerianus* 12 m

Pokaka forms a large canopy tree and is interesting because it passes through distinct juvenile stages, so different from the adult that they are quite unrecognisable. Young plants form a tangled mass of interlacing branches bearing rather scattered leaves that are variously toothed and lobed and appear in numerous shapes. In fact, the variability of the **juvenile leaves** is most remarkable. Generally they are from 1–5 cm long, usually quite narrow and of a brownish green to purplish brown in colour. With age, adult leaves commence to appear on the topmost branches and it then gradually loses its interlacing branches, although they can still persist for many years. The adult tree has a **trunk** up to 1 m in diameter with slightly roughened, pale greyish white **bark**. The **adult leaves** are 3–11 cm long by 1–3 cm wide, their margins being irregularly and bluntly toothed. The white **flowers** are borne on long, slender racemes and are followed by ovoid, purplish **fruits** about 1.8 cm long. Pokaka occurs in lowland to montane forests, in the North Island from about Mangonui southwards and throughout the South and Stewart Islands. It ranges from sea level to 1050 m.

Juvenile foliage.

Narrow-leaved lacebark *Hoheria angustifolia* 10 m

Narrow-leaved lacebark is found in lowland and hilly forests of the North and South Islands from near New Plymouth and Hawke's Bay southwards. Sometimes it will occur as small isolated groves and is often common around forest margins. This species is another interesting forest tree that goes through a distinct **juvenile** stage that is quite unlike the adult. As a young plant it has densely interlaced, twiggy (divaricating) branches and very small leaves. After a number of years it gradually commences changing into its **adult** form. Its **trunk** may be up to 40 cm or more in diameter.

The **bark** is greyish and fairly smooth. Adult **leaves** are 2–3 cm long by up to 1 cm wide, with coarsely toothed margins. The **flowers** are about 1.5 cm in diameter and are produced in clusters of two to five from the leaf axils. In the North Island this species does not have such a pronounced divaricating habit. The inner layers of the **bark** of all hoherias are perforated so that they have a lace-like appearance, and were formerly used for cordage and other ornamental purposes.

Mountain ribbonwood *Hoheria glabrata* 10 m

Mountain ribbonwood is found in the wetter mountain regions of the South Island. It is a small tree, frequently, but not always, branched from the base. Its **leaves** are 5–14 cm long by about 10 cm wide and are toothed around their margins. The leaf apexes are drawn-out into a long point known as a 'drip tip'. Its purpose is generally supposed to facilitate the run-off of rainwater to the ground. The **flowers** of the mountain ribbonwood are 4 cm in diameter and are solitary or in two- to five-flowered clusters from the leaf axils. They are usually borne in profusion in January. Mountain ribbonwood is found in lowland and subalpine forests of the South Island, mainly about and west of the Main Divide. It ascends to 1060 m. It is particularly noticeable on the sites of old slips and avalanche paths where it is one of the first plants to recolonise such areas. The mountain ribbonwood is one of the few New Zealand trees on which the leaves colour in the autumn, when they turn a bright yellow. It is also one of our few deciduous trees.

Mountain ribbonwood *Hoheria lyallii* 6 m

Hoheria lyallii is a smaller tree than *H. glabrata*. It is mainly distinguished from the former species by its branchlets, leaves and flower stalks being densely covered with fine, star-shaped hairs. In fact the **leaves** are so densely covered with these hairs that they usually have a distinctly hoary appearance. They are 5–10 cm long by 2–5 cm wide and are similarly toothed around their margins as *H. glabrata*. The **flowers** of *H. lyallii* are up to 4 cm in diameter and are

produced in two- to five-flowered clusters from the leaf axils. This species is found in montane to subalpine forests, forest margins, streamsides and sometimes along stream terraces in the drier areas east of the Main Divide of the South Island. It occurs from near Blenheim to northern Central Otago and ranges from 360 to 900 m. Some botanical opinion is inclined to merge this and the previous species.

MALVACEAE

Lacebark is quite a variable species and has a number of distinct forms that exhibit a variety of leaf shapes. It has greyish brown **bark** that is slightly roughened. Its **leaves** are from 7.5–14 cm long by 3–6 cm wide and they are rather coarsely toothed around their margins. The **flowers** are up to 2.5 cm in diameter and are produced singly or in five- to 10-flowered axillary clusters, during late summer or autumn. They are followed

by five-winged **seed cases**. This lacebark is confined to the upper third of the North Island from North Cape to the Waikato and the Bay of Plenty. It occurs in coastal and lowland forests and may be common around forest margins and along the banks of rivers. Its Maori name of houhere has given rise to the scientific name of the genus.

Long-leaved lacebark *Hoheria sexstylosa* 8 m

This species of lacebark is found in lowland and lower montane forests, in the North Island from Kaipara Harbour southwards and, in the South Island, to north-western Nelson and Buller to a little north of Greymouth, as well as on Banks Peninsula and near Gore. It ascends from sea level to 760 m and is mainly found around forest margins or in forests. *Hoheria sexstylosa* may have a **trunk** up to 40 cm or more in

diameter. Its **bark** is similar to that of *H. populnea*. The **leaves** may be up to 18 cm long. The **flowers** are up to 2 cm in diameter and are produced singly, or in two- to five-flowered clusters from the leaf axils. It is generally distinguished from *H. populnea* by its narrower leaves and the fewer flowers per cluster. The flowers are followed by **seed cases** with six (occasionally seven) wings. **Young** plants have quite different foliage which is generally smaller and more rounded.

Lowland ribbonwood *Plagianthus regius* 15 m

Lowland ribbonwood is the largest of New Zealand's deciduous trees and its **trunk** may be up to 1 m in diameter. Its **bark** is greyish and with a rather rough appearance. The **leaves** are 2.5–7.5 cm long by 2–5 cm wide and are irregularly toothed and lobed around their margins. The male and female **flowers** are generally borne on separate trees and are in quite large, paniculate cymes, up to 23 cm long. The individual flowers are green to yellowish green and are only 3–4 mm in diameter. **Juvenile** plants of *Plagianthus regius* are quite different and usually have a divaricating stage with quite small leaves. It occurs in lowland forests and is distributed from Mangonui and Kaitaia, in the North Island, southwards to the South and Stewart Island. It also occurs on the Chatham Islands.

Kamahi *Weinmannia racemosa* 25 m

Kamahi is a common tree in many areas and is found in lowland and montane forests, in the North Island, from the mid Waikato and lower Coromandel southwards, and throughout the South and Stewart Islands. It is often one of the commonest trees to regenerate when forest has been cut over. It occurs from sea level to 900 m. Kamahi is a medium to tall forest tree and may have a **trunk** up to 1.2 m in diameter. The **leaves** are 3–10 cm long by 2–4 cm wide. They are quite thick and leathery and their margins are coarsely and bluntly toothed. When in flower the kamahi virtually covers itself so that little foliage is visible. The white **flowers** are produced in racemes that are up to 11 cm long. It is favoured by apiarists for its abundant nectar that produces a distinctly flavoured honey. On **young** kamahi plants the leaves are divided into three leaflets. The foliage from young plants is frequently used by florists, because of its attractive form and reddish coloration. It is then often referred to as 'red birch'. Its timber is attractively figured and has been used for panelling and other purposes, but is seldom used today.

Towai *Weinmannia silvicola* 15 m

This species differs from the preceding because the leaves of adult plants generally have three leaflets, while those of **juvenile** plants have up to 10 pairs of leaflets per leaf. In fact juvenile plants of the towai are almost indistinguishable from *Caldcluvia rosifolia* (see p. 65). Towai has a **trunk** up to 90 cm in diameter. The **leaves** of **adults** are generally three-foliolate, but occasionally may have more leaflets and sometimes may be simple. The leaflets are 4–7 cm long by 2–3 cm wide, thick and leathery, and are coarsely and bluntly toothed around their margins. Its white or pale rose **flowers** are in racemes up to 10 cm long. The individual flowers are only about 3 mm in diameter. Towai is common in lowland forests and around forest margins, in the North Island from Mangonui to Waikato and the Bay of Plenty. Towai is also known as tawhero.

Makamaka *Caldcluvia rosifolia* 12 m

Makamaka forms a handsome, spreading tree with a **trunk** 30–60 cm in diameter. The **bark** is a dark greyish brown and has numerous light brown lenticels. **Leaves** of **juvenile** plants are 7.5–25 cm long and have up to 10 pairs of leaflets, while those of **adults** are somewhat shorter and have three to five pairs of leaflets. The **leaflets** are up to 4 cm long decreasing, in size, downwards, and are sharply toothed around their margins. The small white or pinkish **flowers** are produced in much-branched panicles and are often produced in great abundance. Makamaka occurs only in the North Island, along streamsides and around forest margins in lowland forests from Mangonui and Kaitaia to about Dargaville. It is quite common in the Waipoua Kauri Forest. Its foliage can easily be mistaken for *Weinmannia silvicola*, but is distinguished by having finer and sharper teeth around the leaflet margins.

ESCALLONIACEAE

Putaputaweta is a common species that occurs throughout the three main islands. It is found in coastal to montane forests, and ascends to 1000 m. It forms a small to medium-sized, spreading tree and has a **trunk** up to 30 cm in diameter. The pale greyish **bark** is roughened. **Juvenile** plants have an open habit with zigzagging branches and smaller leaves. The **leaves** of putaputaweta are 2.5–6 cm long by 1.5–3 cm wide, and have a light and dark green marbling on their upper surfaces. Their margins have small, sharp teeth around them. Its small white **flowers** are about 6 mm in diameter and produced in many-flowered, broad and flat panicles up to 5 cm across. Its small, rounded **fruits** are about 6 mm in diameter and are purple-black when ripe. They take up to 12 months to ripen. Putaputaweta is also known as marble-leaf and used to be known as bucket-of-water tree because its freshly cut wood was so sappy that it did not burn easily.

Tawari *Ixerba brexioides* 15 m

Tawari is a beautiful tree that is mainly found in the forest interior, usually growing in the dim recesses of lowland and lower montane forests. It is found in the North Island from Ahipara and Whangaroa southwards to Kawhia and the northern part of Hawke's Bay; ascending from sea level to 900 m. Tawari is a medium tree and has a **trunk** from 30 cm, to sometimes 60 cm, in diameter. Its **bark** is grey and broken into small platelets. Its thick and leathery **leaves**

are 7.5–15 cm long by 1–4 cm wide and have rather coarse and blunt teeth around their margins. In flower it is one of the loveliest of our native trees. The **flowers** are 2.5–3.5 cm in diameter and are produced in five- to 10-flowered panicles. This is one of the few trees for which Maori had a special name (whakou) for the flowers. On festive occasions they were strung together for use as necklaces and garlands.

Westland quintinia *Quintinia acutifolia* 12 m

Westland quintinia is a handsome, small tree that is more widely distributed than its common name would suggest. It occurs in lowland and montane forests in the North Island, from the Great and Little Barrier Islands to the Coromandel Peninsula, and southwards to about the East Cape and central Taranaki. In the South Island it occurs in lowland to higher montane forests from north-western Nelson, and down the

West Coast, to as far south as the Fox Glacier. It is fairly common in South Island forests and generally ranges from sea level to 760 m. It makes a rather bushy tree with a **trunk** up to 60 cm in diameter and has fairly smooth **bark**. Its leaves are 6–16 cm long by 2–5 cm wide and generally have undulating margins with small but distinct teeth. Their upper surfaces are green and shining or often tinged with purplish bronze, while their undersurfaces are quite pale. The small, white **flowers** are produced in long racemes from 5–10 cm long, usually between October and November.

Tawheowheo *Quintinia serrata* 9 m

This species is similar to the preceding, but differs mainly by having narrower leaves, that are not usually wider than 2.5 cm, and it has a more restricted distribution. Tawheowheo is a small, openly branched tree with a **trunk** up to 50 cm in diameter. Its **leaves** are 6–12.5 cm long by 1–2.5 cm wide, and are usually greenish yellow marked with green and reddish blotches. Their distinctly undulating margins are distantly and coarsely toothed, more so than *Q. acutifolia*. The old leaves often turn a bright red before they fall. The **flower** racemes are 6–8 cm long. Tawheowheo is found only in the North Island, from Mangonui southwards to northern Taranaki and Poverty Bay, where it grows in lowland and montane forests. It ranges from sea level to 1050 m.

Kowhai *Sophora microphylla* 10 m

Without doubt, the kowhai is one of the country's most beautiful and widely acclaimed trees. It occurs throughout the North and South Islands, along river banks, around lake shores, forest outskirts and open places in lowland and lower montane regions. It ascends from sea level to 760 m. **Juvenile** plants go through a distinctly divaricating stage which may last for anything from five to 10 years or even longer. This juvenile stage varies from one geographical area to another. Along the dry eastern side of the South Island it is most pronounced and lasts for the longest time. The kowhai may have a **trunk** up to 60 cm in diameter. Its **bark** is rough and furrowed, and greyish or grey-brown. The **leaves** are 7.5–15 cm long and have 20–40 pairs of small leaflets; the leaflets usually being less than 1 cm long. Its **flowers** are up to 4.5 cm long and are produced in four- to 10-flowered racemes. The flowers are followed by four-winged **seed pods** from 7.5–15 cm long. Recent botanical work has resulted in the creation of several new species from what was previously regarded as the one variable species.

This species has a much more restricted distribution, being found only in the North Island, from the East Cape southwards to the Ruahine Range. Like *S. microphylla* it is found along streamsides, forest margins and open places in lowland and hill country, from sea level to 450 m. *Sophora tetraptera* is distinguished from *S. microphylla* by not passing through a divaricating, juvenile stage, and in its much larger

leaflets which are 1.5–3.5 cm long. It will grow into a spreading tree with a **trunk** up to 60 cm in diameter. Its **bark** is greyish brown, rough and furrowed. The **leaves** are 7.5–16 cm long with 10–20 pairs of leaflets. The **flowers** are up to 5.7 cm long and are produced in four- to 10-flowered racemes. Its **seed pods** are up to 20 cm long and broadly four-winged.

Red beech *Nothofagus fusca* 30 m

Red beech is one of the noblest of our beech trees. Its **trunk** may be up to 2 m or so in diameter with shaggy, dark brown **bark**. The base of the trunk is often prominently buttressed. The **leaves** are 2–4 cm long by 2–2.5 cm wide. Around the upper two thirds of the leaf, the margins have six to eight pairs of coarse and sharp teeth. There are separate male and female flowers, although beeches do not always flower well every year. The small **male flowers** are in clusters of one to eight per branchlet, and may be conspicuous because of their yellow or straw-coloured (occasionally reddish) anthers. The **female flowers** are usually in groups of one to five per branchlet. Their **fruits** are small cupules, about 1 cm long, in which sit the nut-like seeds. Collectively, *Nothofagus* are known as southern beeches and also occur in Australia, New Caledonia, New Guinea and South America. Red beech is found in lowland and montane forests from near Te Aroha and Rotorua southwards

to Fiordland and Southland. In the North Island it is (along with other beeches) absent from Mt Egmont. It ascends from sea level to 1060 m. Red beech is also known as tawhairaunui and, in earlier years, as red birch. Its wood is red in colour, straight-grained and is now mainly used for furniture manufacture. The leaves of old trees often turn red before they fall. The foliage of young, seedling trees is usually a deep red, particularly during the winter months. Red beech readily hybridises with black beech and mountain beech.

Silver beech *Nothofagus menziesii* 30 m

Silver beech is one of the most distinctive of the native beech species. It has a dense and bushy, spreading crown, and is easily recognised by its small, hard leaves that are rounded and bluntly toothed around their margins. It makes a tall forest tree with a **trunk** up to 1.8 m or more in diameter. Like the red beech it can develop buttresses around its base. The **bark** of young trees is silvery-white, but with age it becomes grey and rather shaggy. Frequently it is quite heavily covered with mosses and lichens. Its **leaves** are 8–20 mm long by 7–12 mm wide. The young spring foliage is an attractive pale green. The **male flowers** are one to four per stalk and are green to straw-coloured. The **female flowers** are also one to four per stalk and are produced closer to the tips of the branchlets than the males. The fruits are nuts inside small cupules. Silver beech occurs in lowland and montane forests, in the North Island from near Thames and Te Aroha southwards (absent from Mt Egmont), and throughout much of the South Island except in east coast areas. In subalpine areas it often occurs as a stunted shrub. Its wood is deep red in colour, compact and dense, but not well figured. Its main use is for furniture manufacture, although it has been used as a general utility timber. It is also known as tawhai.

Black beech *Nothofagus solandri* 25 m

Black beech occurs in lowland and montane forests, in the North Island, from East Cape and the Mamaku Plateau southwards. In the South Island it is widely distributed as far south as south Westland and South Canterbury. It is absent from Mt Egmont. It ascends from sea level to 760 m. Especially in the South Island it dominates the landscape, covering kilometre upon kilometre of hill or mountain country with its dark green mantle. The black beech derives its common name from the fact that a small scale insect, endemic to the tree, exudes copious quantities of honeydew. This honeydew, in turn, encourages the growth of a black, sooty-mould fungus,

which gives the tree trunk a blackened appearance. The honeydew is a major food source for certain species of native birds. Black beech may have a **trunk** up to 1 m in diameter. Its grey **bark** is rough and furrowed, although on young trees it is fairly smooth. The **leaves** are 7–20 mm long by 4–10 mm wide and have blunt tips. The **male flowers** often have bright red anthers and a tree in full bloom is a remarkable sight. It does not flower well every year. The very small **female flowers** are produced in one- to three-flowered clusters near to the tips of the branchlets. The **seeds** are nuts, 7 mm long, in a small cupule.

Mountain beech *Nothofagus solandri* var. *cliffortioides* 15 m

In most respects this species is similar to the black beech and, with hybridism between the two species, it is often difficult to tell which is which. It differs mainly in being a smaller tree, the leaves having a sharp tip, rather obscure veining and distinctively down-rolled margins. Mountain beech generally makes a small tree with a **trunk** up to 1 m in diameter, but much taller trees sometimes occur. Its **bark** is smooth on young trees but rough and furrowed on old trees. The **leaves** are 1–1.5 cm long by 7–10 mm wide, and clad with a greyish white tomentum beneath. The 1–2 **male flowers** are in groups of three or four per branchlet and often have red anthers. The **female flowers** are produced one or two per branchlet. As with black beech, in drier areas, the trunks of mountain beech are often covered with a black sooty mould. Mountain beech occurs in montane and subalpine forests from the mountains near East Cape southwards, in the North Island, but is absent from Mt Egmont and the Tararua Range. It occurs throughout the South Island and covers many kilometres of mountainsides. Altitudinal range is from sea level to 1220 m.

Hard beech *Nothofagus truncata* 30 m

Hard beech is a tall tree with a **trunk** up to 2 m in diameter, that is often buttressed at the base. The dark slate-grey to blackish **bark** is rough and furrowed. Its **leaves** are 2.5–3.5 cm long by about 2 cm wide. They have eight to 12 pairs of small, blunt teeth around the upper three-quarters of their margins. The **male flowers** are grouped one to three and their anthers vary from greenish to red. Hard beech is found in

lowland and lower montane forests from Mangonui, in the far north, southwards to Nelson, northern Westland and Marlborough in the South Island. It is absent from Mt Egmont. It ranges from sea level to 900 m. Its wood is much harder than that of the other beech species and has been used for railway sleepers, bridge building, posts and poles. It has also been known as clinker beech.

Ewekuri *Streblus banksii* 12 m

Ewekuri is a spreading tree with a short **trunk** up to 60 cm in diameter, and dark brown **bark**. The **leaves** of **juvenile** plants are similar to those of the adult but are often deeply lobed around their margins. **Adult leaves** are 4–8 cm long by 2–3.5 cm wide, and have bluntly toothed margins, which are not lobed. The **flower spikes** are usually produced from the leaf axils and may be solitary, paired or sometimes in threes. The male and female flowers are borne on separate trees. The female flowers are followed by bright red, succulent **fruits**. When the bark of the ewekuri is damaged it exudes a sweetish, milky sap that is palatable. Ewekuri is found in lowland forests from Mangonui in the North Island, southwards to Golden Bay and the Marlborough Sounds in the South Island.

Adult foliage (top). Juvenile foliage (bottom).

Turepo *Streblus heterophyllus* 12 m

Turepo is a small tree found in lowland forests throughout the North and South Islands. It has a **trunk** up to 60 cm in diameter. Its rough **bark** is grey to almost white. It has a long-persisting **juvenile form** of divaricating branchlets and variously lobed leaves that are frequently fiddle-shaped. On **adult** plants the **leaves** are 8 mm–2.5 cm long by 4–12 mm wide, and their margins are bluntly toothed. Their **flowers** are produced on axillary spikes with the sexes being on separate trees. The succulent **fruits** are red. Turepo is also known as milk tree because its milky sap was sometimes used by the early European settlers as a substitute for milk. The turepo is most abundant in moist lowland forests or by the sides of rivers and around forest margins.

Adult foliage (top).
Juvenile foliage (bottom).

Karaka *Corynocarpus laevigatus* 15 m

Karaka is a striking tree with a dense, bushy crown and handsome foliage. It makes a medium-sized tree with a **trunk** up to 60 cm or more in diameter and the grey **bark** is rather smooth. Its thick, leathery **leaves** are 10–15 cm long by 5–7 cm wide and have shining upper surfaces. The small green **flowers** are produced in panicles up to 20 cm long. They are followed by large, orange, succulent **fruits** 2.5–4 cm long. Karaka is abundant in coastal and lowland forests throughout the North Island and in the South Island as far south as Banks Peninsula on the east coast, and Greymouth on the west. It also occurs on the Kermadec and Chatham Islands. Before the advent of European colonisation the karaka was of great importance to Maori. The flesh of the fruit was eaten raw, but the kernels required preparation before they could be eaten, being bitter and unpalatable, but mainly because they were very toxic. They were placed in large umu (ovens) and steam-baked for several hours. The prepared kernels could then be dried and stored for future use.

Kaikomako *Pennantia corymbosa* 12 m

Common in lowland forests throughout both main islands the kaikomako is another tree with a juvenile stage that is quite distinct from that of the adult. **Juvenile** plants pass through a divaricating stage with interlacing branchlets and small, wedge-shaped leaves that are often brownish rather than green. This juvenile stage persists for quite a number of years. The greyish **bark** of mature trees is slightly roughened. The **leaves** are 5–10 cm long by 1–4 cm wide and are coarsely toothed around their margins. Their white **flowers** have a delicious fragrance and are produced in panicles 4–8 cm long. Generally, the male and female flowers are borne on separate trees. The **fruits** are generally black when ripe. Kaikomako occurs from Kaitaia southwards in lowland to hilly forests from sea level to about 600 m. Its hard wood was formerly used by Maori for generating fire by friction. A pointed stick of kaikomako was rubbed along a slab of the softer *Melicytus ramiflorus* or *Schefflera digitata* until a groove was formed. At one end of the groove a ball of fine wood dust would accumulate and eventually could be fanned into a flame.

Matagouri *Discaria toumatou* 2–6 m

Matagouri is a well-known spiny, small tree that is most often seen as a shrub from 50 cm to about 2 m tall. It occurs in both the North and South Islands, but is most abundant down the eastern side of the South Island. It occurs from sea level to about 900 m and is found in coastal areas, open tussock country, rocky hillsides and river flats. In the wet river valleys of the South Island, where the rainfall is high, it frequently forms a scrub forest up to 6 m tall. It is one of the few native plants that has the capability of being able to fix nitrogen in the soil. Its common name of matagouri is a corruption of its Maori name of tumatakuri or tumatakuru. It is also quite commonly known as wild Irishman, presumably because anybody who has to struggle through a thicket of *Discaria* would have the appearance of having been in a fight with a wild Irishman. The gnarled branches armed with sharp spines, up to 5 cm long, make it a most distinctive shrub or small tree. Although it has small **leaves**, in the spring, the stems may be almost leafless at other times of the year. In early summer it produces numerous clusters of small, white **flowers** that are deliciously scented.

Wharangi *Melicope ternata* 7 m

Wharangi is a rather common small tree in coastal and lowland forests of the North Island, and it also occurs in northern Nelson and the Marlborough Sounds in the South Island. It has handsome foliage and has a **trunk** up to 40 cm in diameter. Its **bark** is roughened with small cracks and fissures, and is brown or greyish brown. The **leaves** have three leaflets; each leaflet being up to 7–10 cm long by 3–4 cm wide. The central leaflet is usually the largest. Its small, greenish **flowers** are usually in pairs from the leaf axils and are produced on three-branched cymes. The glossy, black **seeds** are produced in dry, four-lobed capsules. Wharangi often occurs around the margins or in more open parts of the forest. The whole plant is aromatic, especially when the foliage is bruised.

Kohekohe *Dysoxylum spectabile* 15 m

Kohekohe is a handsome and distinctive tree of tropical appearance, with bold foliage unlike that of any other native tree. It also has a character, not uncommon in tropical trees, in that its inflorescences are usually cauliflorous. That is, they are produced from the bare trunk and branches and not from among the foliage. The kohekohe occurs in coastal and lowland forests throughout the North Island, from

North Cape southwards, and in the Marlborough Sounds and adjacent localities, in the South Island. It ranges from sea level to 450 m. Kohekohe has a **trunk** up to 90 cm in diameter. Its **bark** is rather pale and smooth. The pinnate **leaves** are 13–45 cm long by 3–7.5 cm wide and have three to four pairs of leaflets. Its white

flowers are produced on drooping inflorescences up to 30 cm long, during autumn and early winter. The **seed capsules** are up to 2.5 cm in diameter. Due to settlement and the depredations of the introduced Australian brush-tailed possum, it is often devastated and is no longer as common as it used to be. Its wood is said to resemble that of Honduras mahogany and in the past was used for furniture and inlay work.

Titoki *Alectryon excelsus* 10 m

Titoki is found in coastal and lowland forests of the North and South Islands from North Cape to Banks Peninsula on the east of the South Island, and further south in Westland. It tends to favour river flats and sometimes forms isolated groves. It is a handsome tree with a **trunk** up to 60 cm in diameter, and its almost black **bark** is roughened. The **leaves** of titoki are from 10–30 cm long and have four to six pairs of leaflets. Each **leaflet** is 5–10 cm long by 2–5 cm wide. Their margins may be toothed or more or less entire. Its tiny **flowers** are borne on much-branched panicles produced from the leaf axils. The seeds may take up to a year to ripen and are enclosed within a two-valved brown, furry **capsule**. When ripe the capsule splits in two to reveal a jet black seed partially enclosed within a scarlet, fleshy aril, or receptacle.

Akeake *Dodonaea viscosa* 7 m

The Maori name of this small tree means 'for ever and ever', and refers to the very hard nature of its wood which was once used by Maori for making various kinds of clubs. The heartwood is blackish, variegated with streaks of white. It is common in coastal and lowland scrub and forests throughout the North Island and in the South Island to Banks Peninsula, on the east coast, and to a little south of Greymouth on the west coast. Its trunk, and main branches, are covered with a distinctive reddish brown **bark** that peels off (exfoliates) in long strips. Its usually pale to bright green **leaves** are 4–10 cm long by 1–3 cm wide. The small **flowers** are in dense panicles produced from the tips of the branchlets. Frequently the sexes are on separate trees, but some trees are self-fertile. The seeds are produced in attractive hop-like, winged **capsules** that are a distinctive feature of the tree.

Five-finger *Pseudopanax arboreus* 8 m

ARALIACEAE

Five-finger is a much-branched, small to medium-sized tree that is common throughout most forest areas. It occurs from North Cape to about Tautuku in South Otago and to about Greymouth in Westland. It frequently has several main stems and can be recognised by its large leaves with five to seven leaflets, and its large clusters of purplish black fruits. The **leaves** are on stout petioles up to 20 cm

long, and each leaflet is on a shorter petiolule from 1–3.5 cm long. The **leaflets** are 6–20 cm long by 4–8 cm wide, and are coarsely toothed around their margins. The **flowers** are borne in large compound umbels produced from the tips of the branchlets. They are green or purplish and are sweetly scented. Its purplish black **fruits** are flattened and about 5 mm in diameter. The five-finger grows in lowland forests and ranges from sea level to 760 m. It is not infrequently seen growing, as an epiphyte, on tree fern trunks with its roots descending to the ground. It is also known as whauwhaupaku or puahou.

86

Mountain five-finger *Pseudopanax colensoi* 6 m

This species is very similar to *P. arboreus* but the most noticeable difference is that it has only three to five leaflets and they have either no petiolules or are just very shortly stalked. The mountain five-finger forms a small, round-headed tree with stout, spreading branches. The **leaves** are on petioles from 5–20 cm long, and the **leaflets** are 5–17 cm long by 2–11 cm wide. They are coarsely toothed, particularly around the upper halves of their margins. Its **flowers** are similar to those of *P. arboreus* as are its blackish **fruits**. This species comprises at least two varieties, in addition to the typical form (var. *colensoi*) which usually has five leaflets. The typical form is found throughout the North Island and also in the South Island. The variety *ternatus* generally has only three leaflets and occurs throughout much of the South Island and on Stewart Island, while variety *fiordensis* occurs in Fiordland and on Stewart Island. Plants with three leaflets are sometimes known as 'three-finger'. It is also known as orihou.

Pseudopanax colensoi var. *colensoi*.

Lancewood *Pseudopanax crassifolius* 15 m

Especially in its long-lasting juvenile stage the lancewood is one of the most interesting and distinctive of our native trees. **Juvenile** plants have slender trunks clothed with long, very narrow **leaves** (up to 90 cm long) that deflex downwards. They are dark green with yellow or orange midribs and are toothed along their margins. This juvenile stage can last from about 15–20 years before a plant commences to show signs of assuming its adult form. When it begins to assume its **adult** form, branching occurs at its top and at the same time its leaves become progressively shorter. In the mature or adult stage its **leaves** are from 10–20 cm long and they also become broader, being 2–4 cm wide. At this stage the lancewood becomes a round-headed tree. Its **trunk** is distinctively fluted and the grey **bark** is smooth. As with other members of this genus green **flowers** are borne in compound umbels. Its **fruits** are more or less globular and are purple when ripe. The lancewood is common in lowland and lower montane forests throughout the North, South and Stewart Islands, and ascends from sea level to 760 m. It is less commonly known as horoeka.

Adult tree (top).
Juvenile tree (bottom).

Toothed lancewood *Pseudopanax ferox* 6 m

This species of lancewood is not as common as the former and has a rather scattered and localised distribution. It is also a smaller tree. As with *P. crassifolius* it passes through several growth stages.

Its **juvenile** form is similar to that of *P. crassifolius* except that its leaves are shorter, being no more than about 45 cm long. They vary from a dark blackish green to a deep olive green, with orange or yellowish midribs, and their margins are coarsely and harshly toothed. The **adult** of the toothed lancewood is a smaller tree, up to about 6 m, and has a small rounded head. The adult **leaves** are 7.5–15 cm long by 7–20 mm wide and their margins are entire or with a few teeth towards their tips. Its flowers and fruits are similar to those of *P. crassifolius*. It occurs in forest and scrub in the North Island from Mangonui southwards and in the South Island as far south as central Southland. In general, it has a rather scattered distribution. While it is not infrequently associated with limestone areas it is by no means confined to them.

Adult tree (top).
Juvenile foliage (bottom).

ARALIACEAE

Houpara is a handsome small tree that is distributed, in the North Island, from North Cape to as far south as Poverty Bay, but apparently not on the western coast. It usually occurs in forest and scrub near the coast. It has stout, ascending branches. Its **leaves** are on 5–15 cm petioles and have three to five leaflets. The individual **leaflets** are from 5–12 cm long by 2–4.5 cm wide and they have several teeth around the

upper halves of their margins. The green **flowers** are borne in compound umbels produced from the tips of the branchlets. Its **fruits** are purplish and about 7 mm in diameter. In coastal scrub the houpara may be reduced to no more than a shrub. It is also known as houmapara.

Pate *Schefflera digitata* 8 m

Pate is a low-growing tree, usually with several stout, main stems. It has large leaves with three to nine leaflets arranged like the outspread fingers of a hand. The **leaves** are on long petioles up to 25 cm long. Its **leaflets** are 7.5–20 cm long by 3.5–7.5 cm wide and are finely toothed around their margins. On vigorous young plants the foliage presents a particularly lush and subtropical appearance. Its much-branched flower panicles are 20–35 cm across and arise from the branches at irregular intervals. The **flowers** are small and greenish. The globular **fruits** are dark violet when ripe. Pate grows throughout the North, South and Stewart Islands where it is not uncommon in lowland to lower montane forests, from sea level to 900 m. It favours damp parts of the forest, particularly along stream banks. It may also be seen as a roadside tree in some areas.

GRISELINIACEAE

Broadleaf is a very common tree throughout the North, South and Stewart Islands, from near the Bay of Islands southwards. As well as being common in lowland and mountain forests it also occurs in lower subalpine scrub and is often seen in more open situations such as regenerating scrublands and rocky places. It occurs from sea level to 1060 m. It is an easily recognised tree because of its distinctive oval leaves and

rounded, bushy profile. The broadleaf is usually much-branched with a short, gnarled or twisted **trunk** that may be up to 1.5 m in diameter. Its brownish **bark** is rough and furrowed. The **leaves** are 4–7.5 cm long by 2–3.5 cm wide and of a rather thick texture. The minute green **flowers** are produced from the leaf axils, in panicles from 2.5–7.5 cm long. Its fleshy **fruits** are about 7 mm long and blackish when ripe. The wood of the broadleaf is very hard and durable, but is usually too crooked to be used for any but small objects. In the pioneering days it was sometimes used for fence posts. Broadleaf is sometimes known as papauma.

Puka *Griselinia lucida* 8 m

Puka usually commences life as an epiphyte on a large tree such as a rimu and gradually sends a root (or roots) down to the ground. Once that root reaches the ground the puka is then able to grow as an independent tree. The descending roots have quite thick, corky and ridged bark. The **leaves** of the puka are 7.5–20 cm long by 6–12.5 cm wide. They are glossy, bright green, and are markedly unequal-sided at their bases. The panicles of small, green **flowers** are produced from the leaf axils. Its **fruits** are about 8 mm long and dark purplish black when ripe. It occurs in lowland forests from the North Cape to Dusky Sound and Foveaux Strait. It is more common in the North Island and on the west coast of the South Island, and is very local to the east of the Main Divide. It is also known as akapuka.

Neinei is a most unusual and handsome small tree that grows to 7 m or more tall and has a **trunk** up to 30 cm in diameter. The **bark** is rough and peels off in small chips. It has candelabra-like branches with large, rosette-like tufts of leaves at their tips. The long, tapering **leaves**, which are 25–60 cm long by 2.5–4 cm wide, spread and arch outwards. The **flower panicle** is produced from the centre of the leaf tuft and is 15–45 cm long. It bears numerous small reddish **flowers**. The neinei is common in hilly forests of the North Island from Mangonui to North Taranaki and the Mahia Peninsula. It ranges from sea level to 1060 m. Generally, it forms a distinctive element of the undergrowth of kauri forests and is also commonly found along the crests of steep, wooded ridges. It is also known as spiderwood.

Grass tree *Dracophyllum longifolium* 12 m

This is the commonest species of *Dracophyllum*, being found throughout the North, South and Stewart Islands, and also on the subantarctic islands. It is found in coastal, lowland and montane forests as well as subalpine scrublands, and ranges from sea level to 1200 m. It can be quite variable and is quite frequently seen as an erect shrub no more than about 1.2 m or so tall. In forest areas it makes a small tree with a **trunk** up to 40 cm in diameter. It has dark **bark** that is roughened and almost black. The **branchlets** are ringed with the scars of fallen leaves. Its narrow **leaves** are 7.5–25 cm long by 3–5 mm wide and taper to a long point. Generally, they are stiff, although on broader-leaved forms they are often more spreading and inclined to droop. Its white **flowers** are about 8 mm long and produced on racemes 4–5 cm long from the tips of short branchlets. The grass tree is also known as inanga (North Island) and inaka (South Island). Among trampers it is often known as turpentine scrub because of the way that green material flares up when put onto a fire.

EPACRIDACEAE

This is, without doubt, the finest and most outstanding of the native species of *Dracophyllum*. It may have a **trunk** up to 60 cm in diameter and, with its candelabra-like branches and tufts of pineapple-like foliage, it gives an almost subtropical aspect to its mountain habitat. Its peeling **bark** is dark brown. The **leaves** are 30–60 cm long by 2.5–5 cm wide and taper to long points. Its reddish **flowers** are produced on closely and densely branched terminal panicles.

The mountain neinei is found in montane and subalpine forests and scrublands from north-west Nelson, along and west of the Main Divide to about the Haast Pass. It ascends from 760–1370 m. It is sometimes known as the 'pineapple tree'.

Tawapou *Pouteria costata* 7–14 m

Tawapou is a handsome tree that is distinguished by its broad, obovate, shining leaves with parallel veins diverging from the midribs. It also has rather large, bony **seeds** that have smooth and shining surfaces. It is restricted to the upper half of the North Island where it occurs in coastal regions from North Cape to about Tolaga Bay. It is found mainly on the east coast, but also occurs on the west coast from Maunganui Bluff to just north of the Manukau Harbour. It is seldom found far from the sea. It makes a closely branched medium-sized tree and has a **trunk** from 30 to 90 cm in diameter. Its **bark** is rough and varies from brownish grey to grey. Its leathery **leaves** are usually 5–10 cm long by 2–5 cm wide. The small **flowers** are greenish and are usually perfect. Its **fruit** is quite a large berry about 2.5 cm long and varies from yellowish to a deep red when ripe. Maori once used the hard, polished seeds as beads for necklaces. Tawapou was fomerly in the genus *Planchonella*.

Mapau *Myrsine australis* 6 m

Although quite distinct and easily recognised, mapau does bear a superficial resemblance to *Pittosporum tenuifolium*. It is distinguished mainly by its reddish branchlets, pale green or yellowish green foliage and its small greenish or whitish flowers. It forms a small tree with a **trunk** up to 30 cm in diameter. Its **bark** is pale grey or brownish grey. The **leaves** are 2.5–6 cm long by 1.5–2.5 cm wide. They have red petioles

and undulating margins. Its small **flowers** are in crowded clusters, on branchlets below the leaves or in the leaf axils. The male and female flowers are produced on separate plants. The female trees have small, rounded **fruits** that are black when ripe. Mapau occurs in lowland and montane forests throughout the North, South and Stewart Islands. It ranges from sea level to 900 m. It is also known as mapou, matipou and red matipo. Old time bushmen used to refer to it as red maple, the term 'maple' being a corruption of 'mapau'.

Myrsine divaricata 4 m

This is a small tree, although it is not infrequently seen as a shrub. It has a densely
divaricating habit and a most distinctive
appearance. Its main **branches** are stiffly
spreading while the **branchlets** are drooping so that it has a cascading appearance. Its
small **leaves** are 7–15 mm long by 7–10
mm wide, widest above their middles and
shaped like an inverted heart. The minute
flowers are solitary or in few-flowered clusters below the leaves. Its fleshy **fruits** are

about 4 mm in diameter and are violet when ripe. *Myrsine divar-
icata* grows in lowland to higher montane forests and scrublands,
in the North, South and Stewart Islands from Mangonui and
Kaitaia southwards. It is a particularly hardy plant and is one of
the few woody plants to occur on the subantarctic Campbell
Island. It ranges from sea level to 1220 m.

Toro *Myrsine salicina* 9 m

Toro is one of the most distinctive of the native species and is fairly common in coastal to lower montane forests in the North and South Islands from near North Cape to near Hokitika, on the west of the South Island, but is absent from the east coast. It extends from sea level to 850 m. Toro is a small tree usually with a rather slender **trunk**. Its **bark** is very dark red to almost black. The spreading **leaves** are 7.5–17.5 cm long by 2–3 cm wide. Its small, pinkish **flowers** are produced in dense, many-flowered clusters along the branchlets, below the leaves. The succulent **fruits** are about 9 mm long and are a reddish purple or violet colour.

Black maire *Nestegis cunninghamii* 20 m

Black maire is a tall, handsome tree that occurs in lowland forests throughout the North Island and, less commonly, in Marlborough and Nelson in the South Island. Although once quite common it is now rather local in its distribution. It ranges from sea level to 760 m. Black maire has a **trunk** up to 1.5 m in diameter. Its brown or greyish brown **bark** is fissured and furrowed, and of a corky nature. On **juvenile** plants the **leaves** are much narrower than those of the adult, being 15–25 cm long by 8–17 mm wide. The **leaves** of **adult** trees are 7.5–15 cm long by 2–4.5 cm wide and are usually a rather dark green. Its minute **flowers** are produced in eight- to 12-flowered racemes and the male and female flowers are on separate trees. The fleshy **fruits** are 1–1.5 cm long and are red. The wood of the black maire is deep brown, dense and very heavy, and takes a fine polish.

White maire *Nestegis lanceolata* 15 m

This species is similar to *N. cunninghamii*, differing mainly in its smaller size, more slender habit and smaller leaves. It has a **trunk** up to 1 m in diameter and its **bark** is a dark, grey-brown. The **leaves** of juveniles are 7.5–15 cm long by 4–7 mm wide, while those of the adults are 5–12 cm long by 1–3.5 cm wide. Their upper surfaces are dark green and glossy. The minute **flowers** are produced on five- to 12-flowered

racemes that are 8–20 mm long. The male and female flowers are on separate trees. Its fleshy **fruits** are 10–12 mm long and may be orange or red. White maire occurs in lowland and lower montane forests throughout the North Island and in the South Island in Nelson and Marlborough. Nowadays it is of a rather scattered distribution. Its wood is similar to that of the black maire and was used by Maori for manufacturing their ko or digging spades, wooden mere or fighting clubs and various other implements. It was also a favourite fuel for use in meeting houses because it gave a good light and very little smoke.

Oro-oro *Nestegis montana* 15 m

Oro-oro is a smaller, much-branched, round-headed tree with a **trunk** up to 90 cm in diameter. Its furrowed **bark** is a greyish brown. On juvenile plants the **leaves** are 7.5–15 cm long by 4–7 mm wide, while those of the adult are 3.5–9 cm long by 6–9 mm wide. The **flower** racemes are 2.5–4 cm long and are five- to 10-flowered. As with the other species of *Nestegis* the male and female flowers are on separate trees. Its fleshy **fruits** are 6–9 mm long and are red.

Oro-oro is found in lowland and lower montane forests from Mangonui, in the North Island, to Nelson and Marlborough in the South Island. It ranges from sea level to 600 m. Generally, it has a scattered distribution and is seldom seen in any quantity. Its specific name of 'montana' is misleading because it is much more common in lowland forests.

Mamangi *Coprosma arborea* 10 m

Although New Zealand has more than 45 species of *Coprosma* only a few are classified as trees; the remainder are shrubs or sub-shrubs. Mamangi is relatively common in lowland forests of the North Island, from near North Cape to the lower Waikato region. It ranges from sea level to about 500 m. It has a **trunk** up to 40 cm in diameter. The brown **bark** is furrowed and flaky. Distinguishing features of this species are the rounded and shiny leaf blades which have quite broadly winged petioles (stalks) and the dark brown or blackish colour of the young growth. Its **leaves** are 5–6 cm long by 3–4 cm wide. Coprosmas are wind-pollinated with the sexes on different plants. Its succulent **fruits** are about 7 mm long and are white.

Olearia avicenniifolia 2–6 m

This is a common species throughout much of the South and Stewart Islands where it may be seen growing in lowland to mountain scrublands. It quite often colonises road banks and rocky places, and ranges from sea level to 900 m. In exposed situations it is frequently no more than a bushy shrub, but in more sheltered places makes a much-branched small tree with a short trunk up to about 40 cm in diameter.

Its pale **bark** peels off in quite long strips. The **leaves** are 5–10 cm long by 3–5 cm wide and, beneath, are covered with a buff or white tomentum. Its **flowers** are produced in flat-topped corymbs, usually in late summer or early autumn.

Akepiro *Olearia furfuracea* 5 m

Akepiro is a much-branched small tree with a short **trunk** up to 30 cm in diameter and its brownish **bark** comes loose in shreds. As with some other tree species it is often seen as a bushy shrub. The **leaves** are 5–10 cm long by 3–6 cm wide and their undersurfaces are clad with a buff, satiny tomentum. Its white **flowers** are produced in large, flattish corymbs from near the tips of the branchlets. It is found in scrublands, along streamsides and around forest margins and coastal areas of the North Island from near North Cape to the southern Ruahine Range and Taranaki. It ranges from sea level to 600 m. Akepiro is quite common north of East Cape. It is also known as tanguru and wharangipiro.

Olearia lacunosa 5 m

This is one of the most distinctive and easily recognised species of *Olearia*. It grows as a much-branched small tree with a **trunk** 30–40 cm in diameter, or as a shrub. Its **bark** is light to medium brown and peels off in long, ribbon-like strips which may hang on the tree for quite a long time. The **leaves** are 7.5–17.5 cm long by 8 mm–2.5 cm wide. They are thick and very leathery, deep green on their upper surfaces and with a dense, brown tomentum on their undersurfaces. Their margins are obscurely toothed. A further distinguishing character is the prominent veins that branch at right angles from the midrib. The **flowers** are produced in corymbose panicles from around the tips of the branchlets. *Olearia lacunosa* is found in lowland to subalpine forests and scrublands, in high rainfall regions, from the Tararua Range in the North Island to about and west of the Main Divide in the South Island. It occurs at least as far south as the Franz Joseph Glacier. It ascends from about 600 to 1500 m.

ASTERACEAE

Akiraho forms a small tree with a **trunk** up to 40 cm in diameter. In coastal localities it may often be seen as a shrub. Its **bark** is brownish, rough and furrowed. The **leaves** are 4–7.5 cm long by 2–4 cm wide. Their upper surfaces are a yellowish green and they are white to buff-coloured on the undersides. The margins are usually strongly undulating but they may also be almost flat. The delightfully fragrant **flowers** are produced in corymbs that are clustered near the tips of the branchlets. Unusually, for a daisy, each flower head consists of only one floret. Akiraho is not uncommon in coastal lowland areas to lower montane scrublands and forest margins of the North and South Islands from the East Cape southwards to about Greymouth and Oamaru. It ranges from sea level to 450 m. It is also known as golden akeake.

Heketara *Olearia rani* 4–8 m

Heketara is a handsome small tree and, when in flower, often forms noticeable white splashes in bush areas during spring. It is common throughout much of the North Island as well as in Marlborough and Nelson in the South Island. It is usually seen around forest margins, in clearings, and along river or stream banks from sea level to 800 m. It has a **trunk** up to 40 cm in diameter. Its brown or greyish brown **bark** is furrowed and peels off in thin flakes. The **leaves** are 5–15 cm long by 5–6.5 cm wide and are toothed around their margins. Their upper surfaces are green to yellowish green while the undersurfaces are whitish to pale fawn, with prominent veins. Its **flower** heads are about 1 cm in diameter and are produced in large panicles near to the tips of the branchlets. It is one of the most outstanding of the native tree daisies.

This species is the tallest of the New Zealand hebes and will form a much-branched, small tree with a short **trunk** up to 30 cm in diameter. Its grey **bark** is roughened by the scars of old branchlets. On old plants the **leaves** are mainly clustered near to the tips of the branchlets. They are 2.5–7 cm long by about 4 mm wide and have pointed tips. The white **flowers** are produced in dense racemes that are seldom longer than the leaves. *Hebe parviflora* has a scattered distibution, throughout the North Island from about Whangarei (also on the Hen and Chickens and Great Barrier Islands) southwards to the Rimutaka Range, and in the vicinity of Wellington. In the South Island it is known only from eastern Marlborough. It was formerly known as *H. parviflora* variety *arborea* or *H. arborea*.

Ngaio *Myoporum laetum* 10 m

Ngaio is common throughout most of New Zealand, especially in coastal areas, although it also occurs in lowland forests and may extend some distance inland, in river gorges, where air movement prevents damaging frosts. In the South Island it becomes rare and local south of Dunedin, and is absent from Fiordland. It ascends from sea level to 450 m. It is a medium-sized tree with spreading branches, and a **trunk** up to 50 cm in diameter. Its thick **bark** is brown and furrowed. The **leaves** are 4–10 cm long by 2–3.5 cm wide and have finely toothed margins. Their upper surfaces are bright green and shining. Particularly when held up to the light they are dotted with pellucid oil glands. The young leaf buds usually have a blackish appearance. The **flowers** arise in clusters of two to six from the leaf axils. Its fleshy **fruits** are about 8 mm long and vary from pale to dark reddish purple.

111

Puriri *Vitex lucens* 20 m

Puriri is a handsome tree of very large dimensions that occurs in the upper half of the North Island. It is common in coastal to lowland forests from near North Cape to the Waikato region and upper Thames, and then local southwards to the Mahia Peninsula and Cape Egmont. It ranges from sea level to 760 m. It has a large, spreading crown with a **trunk** up to 1.5 m in diameter. Its grey-brown **bark** is furrowed. The **branchlets** are four-angled. The compound **leaves** have

three to five leaflets, the lowermost ones being the smallest. The three upper leaflets are 5–12.5 cm long by 3–5 cm wide and are furrowed along the veins. Its pinkish red **flowers** are produced for most of the year and are borne on branched panicles that arise from the leaf axils. The fleshy, bright red **fruits** are globular and about 2 cm in diameter. Its wood is dark, reddish brown in colour, very heavy and dense and it used to be one of the most valuable of our hardwoods.

Mangrove *Avicennia marina* ssp. *australasica* 2–8 m

Mangrove is a small, much-branched tree that grows in tidal creeks and estuarine areas, sending out special aerial roots that project vertically out of the mud and can be seen at low tide. They are known as pneumatophores and enable the tree's root system to obtain the oxygen that it cannot access out of the estuarine mud. It has grey, furrowed **bark** and stout, spreading branches. Its thick and leathery **leaves** are 5–10 cm long by 2–4 cm wide and their undersurfaces are whitish or buff coloured. The small **flowers** are in four- to eight-flowered clusters on erect, angled stalks. Its **seed capsule** is about 2 cm long. The mangrove occurs from near North Cape southwards to about Kawhia on the west coast, and to Ohiwa Harbour on the east coast. Towards the southern part of its range it is usually no more than a low shrub. It is also known as manawa.

Cabbage tree *Cordyline australis* 4–12 m

The cabbage tree is one of the most distinctive and characteristic of the native trees. It may be seen growing in many different situations throughout New Zealand, varying from swamps to forest margins and barren, windy hillsides. It is found throughout the North, South and Stewart Islands and ranges from sea level to 760 m. When **young** it grows on a slender, unbranched stem and usually has much longer leaves than an adult tree. When it first flowers the flower panicle is produced from the growing tip which causes it to branch. Each successive flowering causes further branching. The cabbage tree may have a **trunk** 10 cm–1.5 m in diameter. Its thick and corky **bark** is rough and fissured. The **leaves** are 30–90 cm long by 3–6 cm wide. Its **flower panicle** is 60 cm–1.2 m long and has numerous, small, white or creamy-white **flowers** that are very sweetly scented. The white or bluish white **fruits** are about 7 mm in diameter. Cabbage trees are quite variable and in some districts may have massive trunks

of very large size, while in others the trunks may be more slender. Particularly in the far north it may have several, very slender main trunks. It is also known as ti-kouka. Ti is a vernacular, generic term for *Cordyline* species. In olden times the pith and fleshy inner root of cabbage tree provided an article of food for Maori, as did the young leaf bud, while the leaves were used for weaving and plaiting.

114

Mountain cabbage tree *Cordyline indivisa* 8 m

This is by far the most handsome of the native species of *Cordyline*, its very broad leaves with their orange midribs immediately identifying it. It has a **trunk** about 15–20 cm in diameter and usually does not form a branched crown. Its thick **bark** is rough and as it flakes off leaves a temporarily smoother surface. The **leaves** form a very large head. They are 1–2 m long by 10–15 cm wide and have thick and prominent reddish or orange midribs. In contrast to *C. australis*, the drooping **flower panicle** is up to 1.6 m long and arises from the trunk, below the foliage. Its **flowers** may be greenish white to purplish white and are densely arranged on the panicle branches. The fruits are about 7 mm in diameter and are a deep, purplish blue. Mountain cabbage tree is not uncommon in the wetter mountain forests from the Hunua and Coromandel Ranges of the North Island southwards and, in the South Island, from Collingwood to Dusky Sound. On the eastern side of the South Island it occurs on Banks Peninsula. It ranges from 450–1200 m. The fibre of the leaves was used for making garments and was said to have been stronger than the universally used *Phormium* fibre. It is also known as toii and broad-leaved cabbage tree.

Nikau palm *Rhopalostylis sapida* 9 m

Nikau palm, being New Zealand's only species of native palm, is very easily recognised, and gives the forest a very subtropical appearance. It is found in coastal, lowland and hilly forests throughout the North Island and, in the South Island, as far south as Banks Peninsula on the east and to Wanganui Bluff on the west. It ascends from sea level to 600 m. Often it is one of the trees that survives after the forest has been cleared. Nikau has a **trunk** 15–24 cm in diameter and is ringed by the scars of fallen fronds. It is smooth, except on very old trees. The **fronds** are up to 3 m long and have a very broad

sheathing base which gives the top of the trunk a bulbous appearance. The **inflorescence** arises from just below the bases of the fronds, is 30–60 cm long and much-branched. The densely crowded **flowers** are a pale, purplish lilac to pinkish colour. Its bright red **fruits** are 12 mm long. Its fronds were formerly used for cladding Maori whares and bushmen's huts while strips from the frond were used for weaving baskets and the like. The unexpanded inner leaf buds as well as the young inflorescences were both edible and eaten in former times.

116

Silver tree fern *Cyathea dealbata* 9 m

Silver tree fern is one of the most distinct and easily recognised of the native tree ferns, the silvery-white undersides of the fronds immediately identifying it. It is from this species that New Zealand's national emblem, the 'Silver Fern' is derived. The **trunk** is up to 45 cm in diameter at the base and is fibrous with the upper part marked by the bases of the old frond stalks. It has numerous **fronds** that usually spread more or less horizontally, and are 2–4 m long by 60 cm–1.2 m wide. The bases of the frond stalks are usually covered with a silvery-white, waxy bloom. On very young plants the undersurfaces of the fronds are green, because the characteristic silvery-white colour does not become evident until the plants are a few years old. On fertile fronds their undersurfaces are dotted with numerous brown **sori**. The silver tree fern is rather common in lowland and montane forests throughout the North and South Islands to as far as the Catlins area, on the east, and is probably absent from the west. Its alternative name is ponga, which is also a generic vernacular name for tree ferns in general. The Maori name of ponga has become corrupted into 'punga' and, sometimes, 'bungie'.

Underside of frond.

Mamaku *Cyathea medullaris* 8–20 m

Not only is mamaku the tallest of our tree ferns, but it is also the noblest, with its tall, slender trunk and huge crown of fronds. It is easily recognised by the more or less hexagonal scars that the fallen fronds leave on its trunk, and by the exceptionally thick, black bases of the stalks of the fronds. Its **trunk** is up to 30 cm in diameter, at the base, but more slender higher up. It has 20–30 **fronds**, slightly curving and from 2.5–6 m long by up to 2 m wide. Their upper surfaces are dark green and shining and the undersurfaces are pale. On the fertile fronds the undersurfaces are dotted with a myriad of dark brown **sori**. Mamaku is found from sea level to 600 m and occurs in lowland and hilly forests throughout the North Island, and in the South Island from the Marlborough Sounds and Nelson down the west coast to southern Fiordland. On the eastern coast, it occurs sparingly in eastern Otago and is rare on Banks Peninsula. It also occurs on Stewart Island. Mamaku is also known as the black tree fern and, on the west coast of the South Island, as king fern.

This beautiful tree fern is abundant in damp lowland and montane forests in the North, South and Stewart Islands from Kaitaia southwards. It ranges from sea level to 600 m and is usually the dominant tree fern at higher altitudes. Its **fronds** have a very soft texture and that, plus the **skirt**, or investment, of the old frond midribs, just below the crown, are its two main distinguishing characters. Strangely, while it does not withstand much exposure to the elements, it occurs on the subantarctic Auckland Islands and has the southernmost range of any tree fern. It has a very matted and fibrous **trunk** about 23 cm in diameter. The **fronds** spread horizontally and are from 1.5–2.7 m long by 45–75 cm wide. They are a bright, fresh green above and paler beneath. The **sori** on fertile fronds are small and dark brown. The whe is also known as soft tree fern and katote.

DICKSONIACEAE

Wheki-ponga is a distinctive and easily recognised species. Its thick, sturdy **trunk** covered with densely matted fibrous roots is much stouter than that of any other native tree fern. If that is insufficient, then the thick **skirt**, or investment, of old, dead fronds, below the crown, should positively identify it. It grows in lowland, hilly and lower montane forests in the North and South Islands, from Tauranga and the mid Waikato southwards, and also on the Chatham Islands. It ranges from sea level to 760 m. The wheki-ponga has a **trunk** 30–60 cm, or more, in diameter. Generally the **fronds** form a vase-shaped crown, and the individual fronds are from 1.2–2.4 m long by 45–60 cm wide. They are quite harsh to the touch, but not as harsh as the following species. The upper surface of the frond is green to dark green and shining, while the undersurface is paler. On fertile fronds the undersurface is covered with numerous brown **sori** which are grouped around the margins of the frond segments and cause them to become strongly down-rolled. Maori

used to use the trunks for the construction of food storehouses, because their thick, fibrous nature made them almost impervious to rats. The early European settlers also used them for the construction of huts.

Wheki *Dicksonia squarrosa* 6 m

Wheki is probably the most abundant of the native tree ferns and it is found in forest areas throughout most of the country. Its main distinguishing characters are the slender black trunk, clad with the hard, black bases of the old frond stalks and the top of its trunk often being girdled with a dense **skirt**, or investment, of dead fronds. Its **trunk** may be 10–15 cm in diameter. The **fronds** are 1.2–2.4 cm long by 60 cm–1 m wide, dark green above and paler beneath. The undersurfaces of the fertile fronds are usu-

ally so densely covered with **sori** that they cause the margins of the frond segments to strongly roll downwards. The black **frond stalks** are densely clad with long brownish black hairs. The wheki is abundant in lowland and hilly forests throughout the North, South and Stewart Islands from sea level to 760 m. It often sends out underground rhizomes that produce new plants so that it frequently grows in groves or colonies. After forest has been cleared, it can be one of the principal regenerative plants, often covering large areas.

Bases of fronds.

Glossary

Alternate of leaves, placed singly along a stem or axis, not in opposite pairs.

Anther the pollen-bearing part of a stamen.

Apex the pointed end or tip of a leaf.

Appressed of leaves, closely and flatly pressed against the surface of a stem.

Aril an appendage to a seed, usually as an outgrowth of the stalk of an ovule, and often pulpy or succulent.

Axil the upper angle, usually between a leaf and a stem; adjective axillary.

Berry a fleshy fruit containing several to many seeds but not a stone.

Bloom a white or glaucous, waxy, powdery covering on some stems, leaves and fruits.

Bract a modified, often much-reduced leaf, especially the small or scale-like leaves of an inflorescence.

Buttress an almost plank-like root occurring at the bases of some trees. Usually found on rainforest trees. Also referred to as a buttress root.

Calyx the outer series of floral envelopes, usually green, each one referred to as a sepal.

Canopy the layer of branches or upper storey in a community of forest trees that forms an almost complete cover over the smaller trees below them.

Capsule a dry fruit which dries out and splits into several parts (valves) when mature.

Cauliflorous (cauliflory) producing the flowers from the old wood of the trunk, branches and branchlets.

Compound particularly of leaves; composed of several, more or less similar parts (leaflets) as opposed to simple.

Cone a general term for the hardened, woody fruits of coniferous trees such as the kauri. They are usually composed of numerous scales.

Corolla the inner, usually showy whorl of floral parts, consisting of free or united petals.

Corymb a more or less flat-topped raceme with the long-pedicelled, outer flowers opening first; adjective corymbose.

Cupule a cup-like structure at the bases of some fruits, especially of *Nothofagus* or southern beeches.

Cyme a broad and rather flat, open inflorescence, flowering from the centre outwards.

Deciduous of trees, shedding all of its leaves in the autumn or, in the case of the kowhais, shedding all or most of its leaves in late spring before new growth commences.

Deflexed bent sharply downwards.

Dioecious having male and female flowers on different plants.

Divaricated with their stiff stems and branchlets spreading at a wide angles so that they become very tangled and interlaced. Usually used for certain shrubs and the juvenile stages of some trees.

Drupe a succulent fruit with the seed enclosed in a stony or bony covering; adjective drupaceous.

Emergent trees that tower above the general canopy area of a forest and are usually scattered so that they appear more as individuals or groups of individuals. See canopy.

Entire mainly of leaves; refers to a continuous margin completely lacking in teeth, although hairs may be present.

Epiphyte a plant that grows or perches upon another plant but is not organically connected to it; adjective, epiphytic.

Fluted referring to the bark of trees; having rounded, shallow grooves or furrows running vertically up the trunk.

Foliolate having leaflets; refers to leaves that have a number of leaflets, e.g. some *Pseudopanax* species.

Footstalk a small supporting stalk often bearing a fruit. In this work mostly used for members of the Podocarpaceae. See aril.

Frond the usually divided (pinnate) leaf of a palm or fern.

Glabrous smooth and hairless.

Gland a minute organ that secretes oil, resin or other liquid, usually on the leaves but may also be on stems and flowers.

Glaucous having a whitish or greyish appearance, but not necessarily due to a waxy or powdery bloom.

Globose rounded or ball-shaped.

Inflorescence the general term for a collection of the flowering parts of a plant, or for the arrangement of the flowers.

Keel the sharp central ridge, like the keel of a boat, often referring to the shape of the leaves of some plants (keeled).

Kernel the edible seed of a nut or fruit within the shell or stone.

Lenticel a corky spot on the bark, of a tree, which functions as a pore or breathing orifice.

Margin the edge or boundary line of an organ, particularly of a leaf but also of the parts of flowers.

Midrib the main central vein of a leaf or similar organ.

Monoecious having separate male and female flowers on the same plant.

Montane of or inhabiting mountain regions. In this work referring to those areas below the subalpine and alpine regions.

Oblanceolate a long and narrow leaf with the broadest part towards the tip.

Obovate inversely ovate or egg-shaped with the broadest part towards the tip.

Opposite particularly of leaves, a pair of organs arising at the same level on opposite sides of the stem.

Ovate shaped like the longitudinal section of an egg, the broadest part being towards the base.

Pakihi open, barren land; used especially for flat, badly drained areas with a distinctive vegetation of fern, shrubby and rush-like plants.

Panicle a loose, irregularly branched inflorescence, usually containing many flowers.

Parted usually expressed as '-parted'; referring to the number of parts of leaves or flowers, e.g. 'five-parted' = having five parts.

Pedicel the stalk supporting a single flower in a compound inflorescence.

Pellucid transparent or translucent dots, or oil glands, on the leaves of some plants, especially those of members of the Myrtaceae.

Perfect a flower having both male and female elements present, both of which are functional.

Perianth the floral envelopes, either the calyx or corolla, or both; used particularly for flowers when the calyx and corolla are not well differentiated in form or one is absent.

Petiole the main stalk of a leaf; adjective petiolate.

Petiolule a diminutive referring to the stalks of leaflets on compound leaves.

Phylloclade a more or less flattened stem that performs the functions of a leaf, particularly on members of the genus *Phyllocladus*.

Pinnate a compound leaf with the parts or segments arranged either side of an axis, or midrib, as in a feather.

Pitting small depressions or pits on the bark of some trees.

Platelets referring to the small plate-like pieces of bark shed by some trees, particularly members of the Podocarpaceae.

Pneumatophore a specialised breathing root of the mangrove (*Avicennia*) that grows upwards from the tidal mud and allows the plant to breath at low tide.

Podocarp a member of the Podocarpaceae family. A very ancient family of predominantly Southern Hemisphere trees.

Pubescent clad in short hairs.

Pungent mainly of leaves; terminating in a sharp, rigid point.

Raceme an inflorescence having several to many stalked flowers arranged along a single stem; adjective racemose.

Rachis the axis, or main stalk, of a compound leaf or inflorescence; plural rhachides.

Receptacle the enlarged, uppermost part of the flower stalk on which the floral parts are borne.

Recurved curved backwards or downwards.

Serrate applied to a leaf having its margin furnished with teeth like those of a saw.

Simple of leaves; in one piece and not being divided into leaflets like those of a compound leaf.

Sorus a cluster of sporangia (spore containing structures) prominent on the fronds of most ferns; plural, sori.

Spike an unbranched inflorescence on which the flowers have no stalks and sit directly on the stem.

Stamen the pollen-bearing organ of a flower comprising the anther and its supporting stalk or filament.

Strobilus a cone-like structure containing the reproductive organs, especially the male or pollen-producing ones. Refers especially to members of the Podocarpaceae; plural, strobili.

Subalpine refers to the lower parts of the alpine zone, above the tree line but below the true alpine zone containing herbfields, fellfields etc.

Subspecies a level just below that of specific rank and above that of a variety.

Terminal borne at the end of a stem and thus limiting its growth.

Tomentum densely matted, woolly pubescence of soft hairs.

Typical form the variety or entity which represents the type of a species on which the name is based.

Umbel a cluster of individual flowers where several flower stalks arise from the same point.

Undulate wavy, having a waved or sinuous margin.

Valve a door-like segment into which some dry fruits split and separate when mature.

Whorled an arrangement of three or more parts or organs, at the same level, around an axis or stem.

Further reading

Allan, H.H., 1961, *Flora of New Zealand*, Vol. 1, Government Printer.

Cave, Y. & Paddison, V., 1999, *The Gardener's Encyclopaedia of New Zealand Native Plants*, Godwit.

Dawson, J. & Lucas, R., 2000, *Nature Guide to the New Zealand Forest*, Godwit.

Eagle, A., 1978, *Eagle's Trees and Shrubs of New Zealand*, Collins.

Metcalf, L.J., 2000, *New Zealand Trees and Shrubs*, Reed Publishing.

Moore, L.B. & Edgar, E., 1970, *Flora of New Zealand*, Vol. 2, Government Printer.

Mortimer, J. & Mortimer, B., 1999, *Trees for the New Zealand Countryside*, Taitua Books.

Poole, L. & Adams, N.M., 1994, *Trees and Shrubs of New Zealand*, Department of Scientific and Industrial Research.

Porteus, T., 1993, *Native Forest Restoration*, Queen Elizabeth II National Trust.

Salmon, J.T., 1997, *The Native Trees of New Zealand*, Reed Publishing.

Simpson, P., 2000, *Dancing Leaves*, Canterbury University Press.

Index